بِسْمِ اللهِ الرَّحْمٰنِ الرَّحِيمِ

Mukhtaṣarul Ḥizbul Aʿẓam

Also including:

- ❖ Mukhtaṣar Ṣalātul Tasbīh
- ❖ Daily Masnūn Duʿās
- ❖ Istikhāra Masnūna
- ❖ Morning and Evening Duʿās
- ❖ Forty Ṣalawāt and Salām
- ❖ Manzil
- ❖ Munjiyāt

Mukhtaṣarul Ḥizbul A'ẓam

A humble appeal is made to the readers for suggestions/corrections to improve the quality of this publication. May Allāh ta'āla reward you for this. The author, translators, editors and typesetters humbly request your du'ās for them, their parents, families, asātiza and mashāikh.

ISBN 13 978 0648247104

Published by:
Firdaws Academy Press
35 Grandview Court, Beveridge
Victoria 3753, Australia
Web: www.firdawsacademy.org.au/press
Email: publications@firdawsacademy.org.au

And when My servants ask you, concerning Me. Indeed, I am near. I respond to the invocation of the supplicant when he calls upon Me. So, let them respond to Me and believe in Me that they may be rightly guided.

Baqarah 186

Arabic Transliteration Guide

Consanants

ء	a/i/u/'	ز	z	ق	q
ب	b	س	s	ک	k
ت	t	ش	sh	ل	l
ث	th	ص	ṣ	م	m
ج	j	ض	ḍ	ن	n
ح	ḥ	ط	ṭ	ه	h
خ	kh	ظ	ẓ	و	w
د	d	ع	'	ی	Y
ذ	dh	غ	gh	ال	al-(article)
ر	r	ف	f	ة	a/at

Short Vowels

َ	a
ُ	u
ِ	i

Long Vowels

ا ی	ā
و	ū
ي	ī

Diphthongs

َو	aw
َي	ay

Honorifics

جَلَّ جَلَالَهُ Jalla Jalāluhu – used to praise Allāh Ta'āla – Meaning may His glory be exalted

ﷺ Sallallāhu 'alayhi wa sallam — Meaning "May Allāh bless him and give him peace." Used for the Prophet Muḥammed ﷺ.

عَلَيْهَا السَّلَام/السَّلَام /عَلَيْهِمُ السَّلَام 'Alayhis salām— used following the mention of a prophet of Allāh, their family or angels translated as, "May the peace of Allāh be upon him/her/them."

رَضِيَ اللهُ عَنْهَا/ / Raḍiyallāho 'anhu/'anhum/'anha —following the name of a companion(s) meaning "May Allāh be pleased with him/them/her."

رَحِمَهُ اللهُ Raḥimahullāh – May Allāh Ta'lā have mercy on him - used for for a pious person.

6

Contents

Translator's Note

All praise is due to Allāh, our creator, nourisher and provider. Peace and blessings be upon all the prophets and upon the last and final messenger Muḥammed ﷺ and peace and blessings be upon his companions who accepted and propagated Islām to the entire world.

This book is a translation of Mukhtaṣarul Ḥizbul Aʿẓam. It is an abridgement of Ḥizbul Aʿẓam which was compiled by the great muḥaddith and Ḥanafi jurist Mulla ʿAli Qāri رحمه الله. It is a collection of duʿās from in the Qurān and Sunna.

On the instructions of Ḥaḍrat Sheikh Mawlāna Zakariyya رحمه الله, Ṣūfi Muḥammed Iqbāl رحمه الله abridged the original in the present form for those busy in tablīgh and taʿlīm activities, so they may derive benefit from making regular duʿās.

This book will benefit any reader. However, it will be easier for those with a good understanding of Islāmic terminology. I have tried to retain as much of the original Arabic words which can not be translated without losing their Islamic spiritual significance.

The Mukhtaṣarul Ḥizbul Aʿẓam is divided into seven sections for each day of the week, starting with Jumuʿa as 'day 1'.

Finally, many people participated in the preparation of this work. I request the readers to remember them in your duʿās and that Allāh Taʿāla accept this work to be solely for his sake.

Khalid Shah

9

Biography of Ḥaḍrat Ṣūfi Iqbāl [1]

Ḥaḍrat Ṣūfi Muḥammed Iqbāl was born in 1926 in the city of Hoshyārpūr, India. He attended a public school. While in sixth grade, he developed a keen interest in dīn and joined a madrasa on his own. After completing the tenth grade, he refused to continue with regular schooling and instead went to Mawlāna Abul Ḥasan ʿAli Nadwi رحمةالله, also known as ʿAli Mian. Unfortunately, he had to leave because of constant illness. Mawlāna ʿAli Mian recommended him to attend Dārul ʿUlūm Deoband. However, his illness returned at Deoband and so once again, he had to discontinue his studies.

He did baiʿa with Sheikhul Ḥadīth Mawlāna Muḥammed Zakariyya رحمةالله in 1945. In 1947, he settled in Pakistan because of his family. In 1963, he migrated to Madīna Munawwara where, in 1970, he started a madrasa for young children named Madrasa Khalilia. He was very close to Sheikhul Ḥadīth who gave him khilāfat in January 1968; he was so devoted to his sheikh that he would spend every Ramaḍān with him in Saharanpūr. He maintained close relationships with many of the notable scholars including Mawlāna Yusuf Dehlavi, Mawlāna ʿAli Mian and Mawlāna Manẓūr Nuʿmāni رحمهمالله.

He was designated by Sheikhul Ḥadīth to write many books such as *Akābir ka Taqwa, Muḥabbat (Achievement of Love)* and *Faiz e Sheikh.*

He breathed his last in the year 2000 in Madīna Munawwara and is buried in Jannat ul Baqiʿ. May Allah ﷻ bless him with His raḥma. Āmīn.

---

1 Biography sourced from www.madania.org, website of Darul Ulūm Madania Buffalo, USA.

Referencing of aḥādīth

For this Mukhtaṣarul Ḥizbul Aʿẓam (Ḥaḍrat Ṣūfi Iqbāl is referring to the urdu version) the translation of Mawlāna Badr e A'alam and the referencing of the aḥādīth from Fatḥul A'azzul-Akram by Mawlāna Abdul Rashīd Nu'māni were relied upon and wherever necessary primary ḥadīth texts were cross referenced for peace of mind. For the virtues of the various du'ās, the books of Ḥaḍrat Sheikh ul Ḥadīth Mawlāna Zakariyya and the footnotes of Ḥizbul A'ẓam by Mīr Sayyid Jamīl Muhājir Madani were consulted. May Allāh give them the highest levels of His pleasure and paradise. And whoever helped in any way in the production of this work, may Allāh reward them and have mercy on them in this world and the hereafter. Āmīn ya rabbal 'ālamīn.

Muḥammad Iqbāl (Madīna Munawarra)

10th of Rabi'ul Awwal 1403 AH

Revised 2nd Dhil Qa'da 1415 AH

Introduction to Mukhtaṣarul Ḥizbul Aʿẓam

Reality of Duʿā

Duʿā is ʿibāda (worship). It is narrated in a ḥadīth that there is nothing more beloved to Allāh ﷻ than duʿā. In another ḥadīth it is narrated that Rasulullāh ﷺ after mentioning the virtues of ʿibāda said that "O slaves of Allāh! Be particular about making duʿā." It is also narrated that when one does not ask Allāh ﷻ, He is displeased with him."

Ḥizbul Aʿẓam

The chosen slaves of Allāh ﷻ are those who make His pleasure the purpose of their lives i.e. they exert themselves in the worship of Allāh ﷻ. These special ones make efforts to do all actions valuable and weighty in the sight of Allāh ﷻ by doing it all purely for His sake (i.e. their actions are not for anyone other than Allāh ﷻ and there is no trace of personal desire). To achieve these qualities of Ihsān (spiritual perfection) and Yaqeen (conviction of faith) they turn to the righteous ʿulamā and special chosen slaves of Allāh ﷻ (usually referred to as a sheikh pl. mashāikh), who themselves have achieved these qualities and understand how to achieve these qualities in the light of the Qurān and Ḥadīth. As Allāh ﷻ has stated "If you don't know, ask the ones who know". So, these mashāikh will then rectify a Muslim's ʿaqāid (beliefs) and aʿmāl (actions) i.e. they will encourage and teach them the pillars of Islam such as ṣalāt, fasting, etc. They will teach them about the ḥalāl (permissible) and ḥarām (impermissible). The knowledge of which is compulsory on every individual. Furthermore, they will be taught certain nafl (non-obligatory) worship and such adhkār (pl. of dhikr – remembrance of Allāh) and ādāb (islamic manners) through which internal purification will be achieved and love for Allāh 羅 will become stronger. So, through continuous remembrance and ikhlās (sincerity) they will be continuously pleasing Allāh 羅.

Among the various Islamic practices that are recited and read is duʿā. Rasulullāh 羅 has mentioned that it is the "essence of worship". He 羅 encouraged making of duʿā and mentioned many virtues and etiquettes of duʿā. Rasulullāh 羅 was the ḥabeeb (beloved) of Allāh and was described as one that was constantly in a state of duʿā. That is why we find in the ḥadīth collections, a huge treasure of duʿās that Rasulullāh 羅 made himself, duʿās that he taught to his nation or duʿās narrated from his blessed companions who were blessed with the Prophet's 羅 companionship and who loved every sunna of Rasulullāh 羅.

May Allāh reward the ʿulamā of this umma who compiled collections of duʿās from reliable sources for the Umma. One of these collections is Ḥizbul Aʿẓam.[2] Sheikhul Ḥadīth Mawlāna Muḥammad Zakariyya رحمةالله used to recite Ḥizbul Aʿẓam as part of his daily routine.

About Mukhtaṣarul Ḥizbul Aʿẓam

During the Ramaḍān of 1401 Hijri, in Stanger, South Africa, Mawlāna Abdul Ḥafīẓ Makki and I were present in a gathering of Ḥaḍrat Aqdas Sheikhul Ḥadīth Mawlāna Zakariyya رحمةالله. He ordered us to prepare an abridged form of Ḥizbul Aʿẓam for those people who are involved in madrasa teaching, tablīgh and

---

2 Ḥizbul Aʿẓam was compiled by Mulla ʾAli Qāri رحمة. He divided the collection into seven parts, one for each day of the week in order to facilitate regular recitation by a person who desires to earn the blessings of duʿā. Imām Jazuli's Dalāil ul Khayrāt رحمة. was derived from Ḥizbul Aʿẓam.

other Islamic works.[3] However he did not specify any principles or method for the abridgment. After much consultation with ʿulamā, this lowly servant selected very concise and easy duʿās and re-arranged the order of those duʿās. In addition, at the beginning, middle and end of each daily reading such ṣalawāt on Rasulullāh 🕌 were added that praise Rasulullāh 🕌 with his noble character and qualities from the book of Allāh ﷻ and the Sunna. By reading these ṣalawāt a person may increase in the love, respect and reverence for the being of Rasulullāh 🕌. To love Rasulullāh 🕌 himself is conditional for imān and without imān and love no deed or imitation of Rasulullāh 🕌 has any value.[4]

How to read Mukhtaṣarul Ḥizbul Aʿẓam

If the following guidelines are revised regularly the importance and value of making duʿā will increase in the heart Insha-Allāh

1. Make duʿā by keeping the purpose of duʿā, its haqīqa reality), its ādāb (ettiquettes) and conditions in the forefront of one's mind, so that the duʿā can be a means of asking, not just to be recited. As for the purpose and reality of duʿā, it was mentioned earlier that duʿā is the essence of worship. For that reason, duʿā should be considered an ʿibāda and it is also the fulfilment of the order of Allāh in the Qurān أُدۡعُوۡنِيۡ "Make duʿā to me".

---

3 Ḥaḍrat Sheikh Maulāna Zakarriyya رحمة الله wanted those engaged in dīni occupations to be also making duʿā on a regular basis. Due to Ḥizbul Aʿẓam's length, he requested a shorter version.

4 Regarding reciting ṣalawāt, the wordings of which are not from the Sunnat, Maulāna Khalīl Aḥmed Saharanpūri رحمة الله has addressed this issue: "It is desirable according to us to send blessings upon Rasulullah 🕌 abundantly and this is among the best of acts and the most beloved of recommendations, whether it is through the recitation of the Dalāil al-Khayrāt and the Awrād of ṣalawāt composed in that book or other texts. However, it is better do so with whatever wording is authentically established from Rasulullah 🕌. However, if one sends blessings using other than what was narrated from Rasulullah 🕌 then that will not be devoid of merit and it will deserve the glad tidings of (the ḥadīth) "Whosoever invokes one blessing upon me, Allāh blesses him ten times." (al-Muhannad)

Introduction

Therefore, duʿā should not be only a way of achieving our needs. It is permissible for the layman to make duʿā for the fulfilment of one's needs and he is also rewarded as well. This does not negate ikhlās. However, for the sālikīn (those who are only seeking nearness to Allāh), duʿā is the expression of their servitude to Allāh. Through duʿā they present themselves in the court of Allāh showing their utter poverty, absolute dependence on Him and make their slavery apparent before Him. Through duʿā they acknowledge his right to be recognised and obeyed as Rabb (Lord) and Mālik (Owner of everything). This is the reality of duʿā. Therefore, it is referred to as the essence of ibāda, even though what caused the person to make the duʿā was some transient need of this world.

2. At the time of making duʿā, one should express a state of desperation, restlessness, humiliation and neediness, even if one must make pretence. The true condition of duʿā is not in our control but we can at least make the appearance of duʿā. That is why Rasulullāh ﷺ has encourages us with these words إِنْ لَّمْ تَبْكُوْا فَتَبَاكُوْ "If you can not weep than pretend to weep". That is make the appearance of weeping before Allāh ﷻ for the sake of Allāh ﷻ.

3. When an appearance of humiliation and neediness is expressed before Allāh then Allāh showers his slave with inner spiritual and external gifts. As Allāh ﷻ says: "ṣadaqas are only given to the fuqarā (destitute)".[5] This is the secret of why sick or hard-pressed peoples' duʿās are more readily accepted.[6]

4. To have conviction that all virtues that are promised for each duʿā will be fulfilled. The greatest virtue (in the Qurān and

5 Tawba 60
6 As we are ordered to give to the destitute, so does Allāh ﷻ give to those who ask like the destitute.

15

Ḥadīth) of sunna duʿās is that we gain the baraka of matching the wording of Rasulllah ﷺ and be able to imitate Rasulullāh ﷺ. Those that imitate the Sunna, they become beloved to Allāh ﷻ.

"Say that if you love Allāh then follow me and He will love you and forgive your sins." 7

Can there be a greater virtue than this!

If we also keep in mind the virtues of each duʿā, this will create delight, enthusiasm and ikhlās while we make those duʿās.

5. We should not miss any duʿā which is part of our regular routine because His being our lord and we being his slaves is a continuous condition. Allāh is always rabb (lord) and slaves are always in need of their rabb.

6. Duʿās should not simply be read but should be recited while one is beseeching and imploring Allāh ﷻ. Sometimes, the translation should be read so it is known for what need the duʿā is being made. When one reflects on these duʿās, yaqīn on the oneness of Allāh ﷻ is created, our own helplessness and neediness becomes apparent, purification of the inner-self takes place and love for virtue and aversion to vice increases. It is only natural that something a person desires from the heart will induce him to make practical effort to achieve that thing.

The etiquettes of duʿā, special places and times when duʿā is more readily accepted such as the sixteen places in Makka Mukarrama are written in the book Ḥisn Ḥasīn. We should read

7 Āl Imrān 31

them every now and then. For the sake of brevity, I have not enumerated them here.

8. By the kindness of Allāh ﷻ if a slave of Allāh has desire to make abundant du'ā. Then du'ās should not be restricted to the daily ḥizb. One should try to read the whole book or as much as possible. When you are being given the ability by Allāh to be able to present your needs before Him, then these moments should be capitalised.

9. It is not against istiqāma or steadfastness to read more than the usual amount on certain days such as Ramaḍān or on holidays to temporarily increase the amount and then to leave it. However, it is better that one should reduce the daily amount but do it on a more continuous basis.

Every week, one or two translations of du'ās and their virtues should be memorised. Then after the five times ṣalāt and at various other times, these du'ās should be repeated, so the fayḍ (grace) and spiritual state associated with that du'ā is achieved. The gist and the essence of the meaning of the du'ā should be coupled with emotion in the heart.

Note

In the beginning, the previously mentioned points should be actively remembered. However, over time these matters will become natural and such an aptitude will be acquired that whenever these du'ās will be made, their virtues and meanings will instinctively be recalled. This is due to divine help

Mukhtaṣarul Ḥizbul A'ẓam – Day One - Jumuʿa

Day One - Jumuʿa

1

بِسْمِ اللهِ الرَّحْمٰنِ الرَّحِيْمِ

اَلْحَمْدُ لِلّٰهِ رَبِّ الْعٰلَمِيْنَ ۞ الرَّحْمٰنِ الرَّحِيْمِ ۞ مٰلِكِ يَوْمِ الدِّيْنِ ۞ إِيَّاكَ نَعْبُدُ وَإِيَّاكَ نَسْتَعِيْنُ ۞ اِهْدِنَا الصِّرَاطَ الْمُسْتَقِيْمَ ۞ صِرَاطَ الَّذِيْنَ أَنْعَمْتَ عَلَيْهِمْ غَيْرِ الْمَغْضُوْبِ عَلَيْهِمْ وَلَا الضَّآلِّيْنَ ۞

In the name of Allāh, the Most Gracious, the Most Merciful

All praise is due to Allāh, Lord of the worlds. The Most Gracious, the Most Merciful. Sovereign of the Day of Judgment. You alone we worship, and You alone we ask for help. Guide us to the straight path; The path of those upon whom You have bestowed Your grace, not of those who have incurred Your wrath, nor of those who have gone astray.

❖ Here Sura Fātiha is recited with the intention of praising Allāh and duʿā. Therefore, a menstruating woman or a person who is junub (requiring a ritual bath) can also read it.[8] However, they should not touch the writing in the book

---

8 Raddul Mukhtār p. 302

❖ It has been narrated in a ḥadīth that Sura Fātiha is cure for all ailments.[9] This sura is more virtuous then two thirds of the Qurān.[10] The mashāikh have written that those who read this sura with imān and yaqīn, it is shifā' (cure) for all sicknesses. Whether they be related to dīn, dunya, inwardly spiritual or outwardly physical.

❖ Within the verse اِيَّاكَ نَعْبُدُ وَاِيَّاكَ نَسْتَعِينُ "You alone we worship, and You alone we ask for help" is contained our wordly and spiritual needs and goals." [11] The secret of why this ayat is a means of achieving shifā and all other goals is that it contains pure tawheed (oneness of Allāh).[12]

2

اَللّٰهُمَّ صَلِّ وَسَلِّمْ اَشْرَفَ الصَّلٰوةِ وَالتَّسْلِيْمِ عَلٰى حَبِيْبِكَ سَيِّدِنَا وَ

نَبِيِّنَا مُحَمَّدٍ عَبْدِكَ وَرَسُوْلِكَ نَبِيِّ الرَّحْمَةِ الَّذِيْ اَمَرْتَ الْمُؤْمِنِيْنَ

بِالصَّلٰوةِ وَالسَّلَامِ عَلَيْهِ فِيْ كِتَابِكَ فَبَدَأْتَ بِالصَّلٰوةِ عَلَيْهِ بِنَفْسِكَ وَ

ثَنَّيْتَ بِمَلَائِكَتِكَ فَقُلْتَ يَا مَنْ جَلَّ شَأْنُكَ ﴿ اِنَّ اللهَ وَمَلَائِكَتَهُ

يُصَلُّوْنَ عَلَى النَّبِيِّ يَآ اَيُّهَا الَّذِيْنَ آمَنُوْا صَلُّوْا عَلَيْهِ وَسَلِّمُوْا تَسْلِيْمًا ﴾

الاحزاب

---

9 Dārimi
10 Faḍāil Qurān
11 Faḍāil Qurān
12 Zādul Ma'ād

O Allāh! Confer the noblest peace and blessings on your beloved, our master and prophet, the prophet of mercy, as you ordered the believers to confer peace and blessings upon him and you started with your self in your book and then ordered the angels to also send peace and blessings. O the One whose status is exalted! You have yourself said ""Verily, Allāh and His angels shower blessings on the Prophet. O Believers! Send blessings upon him and salute him with a worthy salutation". [13]

This noble ṣalāt[14] contains a Qurānic verse which explicitly orders the believers to send ṣalāt and salām on the holy Prophet ﷺ. This action is important and beloved to Allāh ﷻ because Allāh ﷻ himself sent ṣalāt and salām upon him. Therefore, the unique status of Rasulullāh ﷺ before Allāh ﷻ becomes evident that he is a favoured, honoured and loved one of Allāh ﷻ. No other form of worship has been ordered in a similar manner i.e. Allāh ﷻ himself doing ṣalāt on Rasulullāh ﷺ and ordering us to do the same.

3

اَللّٰهُمَّ اجْعَلْ صَلَوَاتِكَ وَرَحْمَتَكَ وَبَرَكَاتِكَ عَلٰى سَيِّدِ الْمُرْسَلِيْنَ وَ إِمَامِ الْمُتَّقِيْنَ وَخَاتَمِ النَّبِيِّيْنَ مُحَمَّدٍ عَبْدِكَ وَرَسُوْلِكَ إِمَامِ الْخَيْرِ وَقَائِدِ الْخَيْرِ وَرَسُوْلِ الرَّحْمَةِ

---

13 Qurān - 33:56

14 When one takes the name of Rasulullah ﷺ he is required to send salat & salam upon him. (Surah Ahzab, verse: 56) Salat is translated as: salutations, and salam as: peace. Salat is generally sent with the words: صَلَّى اللهُ عَلَيْهِ and salam is sent with the words: وَسَلَّمَ (hadithanswers.com)

اَللّٰهُمَّ ابْعَثْهُ مَقَامًا مَّحْمُوْدًا تَّحْمِدُهُ بِهِ الْأَوَّلُوْنَ وَالْآخِرُوْنَ

اَللّٰهُمَّ صَلِّ عَلٰى مُحَمَّدٍ وَّعَلٰى آلِ مُحَمَّدٍ كَمَا صَلَّيْتَ عَلٰى إِبْرَاهِيْمَ وَعَلٰى

آلِ إِبْرَاهِيْمَ إِنَّكَ حَمِيْدٌ مَّجِيْدٌ اَللّٰهُمَّ بَارِكْ عَلٰى مُحَمَّدٍ وَّعَلٰى آلِ مُحَمَّدٍ

كَمَا بَارَكْتَ عَلٰى إِبْرَاهِيْمَ وَعَلٰى آلِ إِبْرَاهِيْمَ إِنَّكَ حَمِيْدٌ مَّجِيْدٌ

O Allāh! Descend your special gifts, mercies and blessings upon the master of the messengers, the imām of the righteous and the seal of the Prophets; Muḥammad your slave, messenger, the imām of virtues, the leader of good and messenger of mercy (whose existence is a mercy for worlds). O Allāh! Raise him to the Praised Station which is the envy of the first ones and the last ones. O Allāh! Confer blessings upon Muḥammad and upon the family of Muḥammad in the manner You conferred blessings upon Ibrāhīm. Verily, You are the Praiseworthy, the Majestic. O Allāh, bless Muḥammad and the family of Muḥammad in the manner You blessed Ibrāhīm. Verily, You are the Praiseworthy, the Majestic.

Ḥaḍrat ʿAbdullah Ibn Masʿūd ﷺ said that whenever you wish to send ṣalāt on the Prophet ﷺ then do so in the best possible way because this ṣalāt will be presented to Rasulullāh ﷺ. The people asked "tell us the best possible way to send ṣalāt." So, he then taught them the above.[15]

---

15 Ibn Māja

4

اَللّٰهُمَّ صَلِّ عَلٰى مُحَمَّدٍ النَّبِيِّ وَأَزْوَاجِهٖ أُمَّهَاتِ الْمُؤْمِنِيْنَ وَذُرِّيَّتِهٖ وَأَهْلِ بَيْتِهٖ كَمَا صَلَّيْتَ عَلٰى إِبْرَاهِيْمَ إِنَّكَ حَمِيْدٌ مَّجِيْدٌ

O Allāh! Confer blessings upon Muḥammad, the unlettered Prophet and upon his wives, the mothers of the Believers, upon his progeny and his household just as you conferred blessings upon Ibrāhīm. Verily, You are the Praiseworthy, the Majestic.

Ḥaḍrat Abu Hurayra ﷠ has narrated that Rasulullāh ﷺ said who ever desires that his deeds be weighed in very large scales (meaning to be rewarded greatly) should recite this ṣalāt on the Prophet ﷺ and his household.[16]

5

اَللّٰهُمَّ صَلِّ عَلٰى مُحَمَّدٍ وَّأَنْزِلْهُ الْمَقْعَدَ الْمُقَرَّبَ عِنْدَكَ يَوْمَ الْقِيَامَةِ

O Allāh! Confer blessings upon Muḥammad and bestow upon him the station of proximity to You on the Day of Judgement.

Ḥaḍrat Ruwayfiʿ ﷠ has narrated from Rasulullāh ﷺ that whosoever recites the above ṣalāt, Rasulullāh's intercession will be incumbent for him.[17]

---

16 Abu Dawūd via Faḍāil Durūd
17 Faḍāil Durūd

6

اَللّٰهُمَّ صَلِّ عَلٰى (سَيِّدِنَا) مُحَمَّدٍ وَّعَلٰى آلِ (سَيِّدِنَا) مُحَمَّدٍ كَمَا تُحِبُّ

وَتَرْضٰى لَهٗ

O Allāh! Confer blessings upon (our master) Muḥammad and upon the family of (our master) Muḥammad in the manner that you love and are pleased with for him.

Rasulullāh ﷺ has especially honoured the reciter of this ṣalāt by seating him near himself. On seeing this, Sahāba ؓ were amazed. Rasulullāh ﷺ said that this person recited the above ṣalāt upon him.[18]

7

اَللّٰهُمَّ صَلِّ عَلٰى (سَيِّدِنَا) مُحَمَّدٍ وَّ أَبْلِغْهُ الْوَسِيلَةَ وَ الدَّرَجَةَ الرَّفِيعَةَ مِنَ

الْجَنَّةِ اَللّٰهُمَّ اجْعَلْ فِي الْمُصْطَفَيْنَ مَحَبَّتَهُ وَفِي الْمُقَرَّبِيْنَ مَوَدَّتَهُ وَفِي

الْأَعْلَيْنَ ذِكْرَهُ وَ السَّلَامُ عَلَيْهِ وَ رَحْمَةُ اللّٰهِ وَبَرَكَاتُهُ

O Allāh! Confer blessings upon (our master) Muḥammad, and make him reach the wasīla and and the loftiest Paradise. O Allāh place his love in (your) chosen ones' (hearts) and place sincere affection for him in (your) close one's (hearts) and place his remembrance in

---

18 Al-Qawlul Badīʿ

(your) eminent ones' (hearts). May peace, mercy and blessings be upon him.

This ṣalāt upon the Prophet has been narrated by Ḥaḍrat Abdullah bin Masʿūd ؓ. In another narration it is stated that the person who asks Allāh for the *wasīla* for me (the highest status in Paradise or to become the beloved of Allāh) then my intercession will descend upon him. In another narration it is said that my intercession will become incumbent for him.[19]

8

اَللّٰهُمَّ صَلِّ عَلٰى رُوحِ (سَيِّدِنَا) مُحَمَّدٍ فِي الْأَرْوَاحِ اَللّٰهُمَّ صَلِّ عَلٰى جَسَدٍ (سَيِّدِنَا) مُحَمَّدٍ فِي الْأَجْسَادِ اَللّٰهُمَّ صَلِّ عَلٰى قَبَرٍ (سَيِّدِنَا) مُحَمَّدٍ فِي الْقُبُوْرِ

O Allāh! Confer blessings upon the soul of (our master) Muḥammad amongst all souls. O Allāh, confer blessings upon the body of (our master) Muḥammad amongst all bodies. O Allāh, confer blessings upon the grave of (our master) Muḥammad amongst all graves.

In Qawlul Badīʿ a narration from Rasulullāh ﷺ states that "Whoever reads this ṣalāt will see me in a dream and I will do his intercession and whoever I intercede for, he will drink from my Ḥawḍ (the great pond of Kawthar on the Day of Judgement) and will forbid the fire of Jahannam on him."[20]

---

19 Faḍāil Durūd
20 Faḍāil Durūd

Experience has shown that if someone wants to see Rasulullāh ﷺ in a dream, one should be in a state of wuḍu and read this ṣalāt at the time of sleeping seventy times. And then the following ṣalāt should also be read.

9

اَللّٰهُمَّ صَلِّ عَلٰى (سَيِّدِنَا) مُحَمَّدٍ كُلَّمَا ذَكَرَهُ الذَّاكِرُوْنَ وصَلِّ عَلٰى
(سَيِّدِنَا) مُحَمَّدٍ كُلَّمَا غَفَلَ عَنْ ذِكْرِهِ الْغَافِلُوْنَ

O Allāh! Confer blessings on (our master) Muḥammad whenever he is remembered by those who remember him, and confer blessings on (our master) Muḥammad and family whenever he is not remembered by the negligent.

Imam Shāfiʿi رحمه الله used to do ṣalāt in this manner. Someone saw him in dream. He said that Allāh ﷻ forgave me because of this ṣalāt.[21]

10

اَللّٰهُمَّ صَلِّ عَلٰى (سَيِّدِنَا) مُحَمَّدٍ وَّعَلٰى آلِ (سَيِّدِنَا) مُحَمَّدٍ صَلٰوةً تَكُوْنُ
لَكَ رِضًى وَّلِحَقِّهِ أَدَآءً وَّ اَعْطِهِ الْوَسِيْلَةَ وَالْمَقَامَ الْمَحْمُوْدَ الَّذِيْ وَعَدْتَّهُ وَ

---

21 Al Qawlul Badīʿ

اجْزِهِ عَنَّا مَا هُوَ أَهْلُهُ وَ اجْزِهِ عَنَّا مِنْ أَفْضَلِ مَا جَزَيْتَ نَبِيًّا عَنْ أُمَّتِهِ وَ

صَلِّ عَلَى جَمِيعِ إِخْوَانِهِ مِنَ النَّبِيِّيْنَ وَ الصَّالِحِيْنَ يَا أَرْحَمَ الرَّاحِمِيْنَ

O Allāh! Confer blessings upon (our master) Muḥammad and the
family of (our master) Muḥammad, blessings which You are pleased
with, which fulfil his rights, and grant him the wasīla and the
Praised Station you have promised him. Reward him on our behalf
with a reward he deserves. Reward him on our behalf with the best
You have ever rewarded any prophet on behalf of his followers.
Confer blessings upon him and all his brothers from among the
prophets and the pious, O Most Merciful of those who show mercy.

It is narrated from Rasulullāh ﷺ that whoever reads this ṣalāt
seven times for seven Jumuaʿhs then my intercession will be
incumbent for him.[22]

11

اَللّٰهُمَّ صَلِّ عَلَى (سَيِّدِنَا) مُحَمَّدٍ عَبْدِكَ وَرَسُوْلِكَ وَصَلِّ عَلَى الْمُؤْمِنِيْنَ

وَالْمُؤْمِنَاتِ وَالْمُسْلِمِيْنَ وَالْمُسْلِمَاتِ

O Allāh! Confer blessings upon (our master) Muḥammad, your
servant and your Messenger, and confer blessings upon the believing
men and the believing women, the Muslim men and Muslim women.

---

22 Al Qawlul Badīʾ

27

Rasulullāh ﷺ has said that whichever Muslim does not have anything to give in sadaqa should say this ṣalāt. This shall be a zakāt (charity and a means of purification) for this person.[23]

12

إِنَّ اللهَ وَمَلٰٓئِكَتَهٗ يُصَلُّوْنَ عَلَى النَّبِيِّ ۭ يٰٓاَيُّهَا الَّذِيْنَ اٰمَنُوْا

صَلُّوْا عَلَيْهِ وَسَلِّمُوْا تَسْلِيْمًا ۞ لَبَّيْكَ اَللّٰهُمَّ رَبِّيْ وَسَعْدَيْكَ صَلَوَاتُ

اللهِ الْبَرِّ الرَّحِيْمِ وَالْمَلَائِكَةِ الْمُقَرَّبِيْنَ وَ النَّبِيِّيْنَ وَ الصِّدِّيْقِيْنَ وَ

الشُّهَدَآءِ وَ الصَّالِحِيْنَ وَمَا سَبَّحَ لَكَ مِنْ شَيْءٍ يَا رَبَّ الْعَالَمِيْنَ عَلٰى سَيِّدِنَا

مُحَمَّدِ بْنِ عَبْدِ اللهِ خَاتَمِ النَّبِيِّيْنَ وَسَيِّدِ الْمُرْسَلِيْنَ وَ إِمَامِ الْمُتَّقِيْنَ وَ

رَسُوْلِ رَبِّ الْعَالَمِيْنَ الشَّاهِدِ الْبَشِيْرِ الدَّاعِي إِلَيْكَ بِاِذْنِكَ السِّرَاجِ

الْمُنِيْرِ وَعَلَيْهِ السَّلَامُ

Verily, Allāh and His angels confer blessings on the Prophet. O Believers! Confer blessings upon him and salute him with a worthy salutation

At Your service O Allāh! My Lord, and ready to serve! May the blessings of Allāh, the Kind, the Most Merciful, and the near angels, the Prophets, the immensely true ones, the martyrs, the righteous and

---

23 Al Qawlul Badī'

whatever glorifies You, O Lord of the worlds, be upon our master Muḥammad son of ʿAbdullah, the Seal of the Prophets, and the master of the Messengers, the Imām of those who fear Allāh and the Messenger of the Lord of the worlds, the Witness, bringer of good tidings, the one who calls to You with Your permission, the luminous lamp, and peace be upon him.

Ḥaḍrat ʿAli ؓ said that he used to read ṣalāt in this manner and that he recited the same during the funeral prayers of Rasulullāh ﷺ and taught it to others as well.[24]

13

وَأَعۡطِهِ سُؤۡلَهُ فِي آخِرَةِ وَالۡأُوۡلٰى كَمَا آتَيۡتَ إِبۡرَاهِيۡمَ وَمُوۡسٰى ۚ اَللّٰهُمَّ تَقَبَّلۡ شَفَاعَةَ (سَيِّدِنَا) مُحَمَّدٍ الۡكُبۡرٰى وَارۡفَعۡ دَرَجَتَهُ الۡعُلۡيَا

O Allāh! Accept the greatest intercession of (our master) Muḥammad and raise his high degree, and give him what he asks for in the hereafter and this world as You did for Ibrāhīm ؑ and Musa ؑ.

This ṣalāt has been narrated from Ḥaḍrat ʿAbdullah Ibn ʿAbbās ؓ.[25]

14

اَللّٰهُمَّ صَلِّ عَلٰى (سَيِّدِنَا) مُحَمَّدٍ وَعَلٰى آلِ (سَيِّدِنَا) مُحَمَّدٍ

---

24 Maʾāriful Ḥadīth
25 Al Qawlul Badīʾ

29

وَّأَصْحَابِهِ وَأَوْلَادِهِ وَأَهْلِ بَيْتِهِ وَذُرِّيَّتِهِ وَمُحِبِّيْهِ وَأَتْبَاعِهِ وَأَشْيَاعِهِ

وَعَلَيْنَا مَعَهُمْ أَجْمَعِيْنَ يَا أَرْحَمَ الرَّاحِمِيْنَ

O Allāh! Confer your blessings upon (our master) Muḥammad, and upon (our master) Muḥammad's family, his companions, his children, his household, his progeny, those who love him, his followers, his adherents and upon us with all of them, O Most Merciful of those who show mercy.

This ṣalāt is narrated from Imām Ḥasan Baṣri ﷫.[26] He used to recite it as well.

15

اَللّٰهُمَّ صَلِّ عَلٰى (سَيِّدِنَا) مُحَمَّدٍ وَّ عَلٰى آلِ (سَيِّدِنَا) مُحَمَّدٍ وَّ

هَبْ لَنَا اَللّٰهُمَّ ارْزُقْنَا مِنْ رِزْقِكَ الْحَلَالِ الطَّيِّبِ الْمُبَارَكِ مَا تَصُوْنُ بِهِ

وُجُوْهَنَا عَنِ التَّعَرُّضِ إِلٰى أَحَدٍ مِّنْ خَلْقِكَ

O Allāh! Confer your blessings upon (our master) Muḥammad, and upon the family of (our master) Muḥammad and bless us also. O Allāh, grant us such halal and pure sustenance full of blessing that we are saved from turning to any of your creation (as beggars).

---

26 Al Qawlul Badīʿ

Once Abu ʿAbdullah Qastalāni رَحِمَهُ اللّٰه saw Rasulullāh ﷺ in his dream. He complained to Rasulullāh ﷺ of his poverty. He ﷺ instructed him to read this ṣalāt.

16

اَللّٰهُمَّ اغْفِرْ لِلْمُؤْمِنِيْنَ وَالْمُؤْمِنَاتِ وَالْمُسْلِمِيْنَ وَالْمُسْلِمَاتِ الْاَحْيَآءِ مِنْهُمْ وَالْاَمْوَاتِ وَلِاِخْوَانِنَا الَّذِيْنَ سَبَقُوْنَا بِالْاِيْمَانِ وَلَا تَجْعَلْ فِيْ قُلُوْبِنَا غِلًّا لِلَّذِيْنَ اٰمَنُوْا رَبَّنَا اِنَّكَ رَءُوْفٌ رَّحِيْمٌ ۞

O Allāh! Forgive all the believing men and all the believing women, all the Muslim men and all the Muslim women, those alive and those who have passed away, and those of our brothers who preceded us in faith and put not in our hearts any grudge toward those who have believed. Our Lord, indeed You are Kind and Merciful.

After making ṣalawāt, it is an oppurtunuity to have duʿās accepted. Therefore, one should make duʿā such as the above one for one's own forgiveness and the forgiveness of the whole umma. Also, this ends with a duʿā (from the Qurān) which removes any grudges from our hearts.

17

اَللّٰهُمَّ صَلِّ عَلٰى (سَيِّدِنَا) مُحَمَّدٍ عَبْدِكَ وَنَبِيِّكَ وَرَسُوْلِكَ النَّبِيِّ الْاُمِّيِّ

O Allāh! Confer blessings upon (our master) Muḥammad, Your servant, Your Prophet and Your Messenger, the unlettered Prophet.

It is transmitted in a ḥadīth that the noble Prophet ﷺ said, "Whoever confers blessings upon me eighty times on Jumuʿa, eighty years of his sins will be forgiven." A person asked, "O Messenger of Allāh, how should we confer blessings?" The Noble Prophet ﷺ taught him the above ṣalāt and said "Close one finger after saying this (i.e. count using your fingers)."[27] It is not a condition to do so after the ʿAsr prayers on Jumuʿa.

18

اَللّٰهُمَّ صَلِّ وَسَلِّمْ وَبَارِكْ عَلٰى رُوْحِ سَيِّدِنَا مُحَمَّدٍ فِي الْأَرْوَاحِ وَصَلِّ وَسَلِّمْ عَلٰى قَلْبِ سَيِّدِنَا مُحَمَّدٍ فِي الْقُلُوْبِ وَصَلِّ وَسَلِّمْ عَلٰى جَسَدِ سَيِّدِنَا مُحَمَّدٍ فِي الْأَجْسَادِ وَصَلِّ وَسَلِّمْ عَلٰى قَبْرِ سَيِّدِنَا مُحَمَّدٍ فِي الْقُبُوْرِ

O Allāh! Confer blessings and salutations upon, and bless the soul of our master Muḥammad from amongst all souls. Confer blessings and salutations upon the heart of our master Muḥammad amongst all hearts. Confer blessings and salutations upon the body of our master Muḥammad amongst all bodies. Confer blessings and salutations upon the grave of our master Muḥammad amongst all graves."

A certain wali of Allāh (or friend of Allāh) was suffering from an illness. He saw Shaykh Shihābuddīn bin Raslān رَحِمَهُ اللهُ, a great ascetic and scholar, in his dream. He complained about his illness to the shaykh. The Shaykh said, "How is it that you are oblivious to the tried and tested antidote? He then advised him to recite the above ṣalāt. After seeing this dream, he began

---

27 Faḍāil Durūd sourced from Dār Qutni

conferring this ṣalāt in abundance and thus his illness was cured.[28]

19

اَللّٰهُمَّ اِنَّا نَسْئَلُكَ مِنْ خَيْرِ مَا سَئَلَكَ مِنْهُ نَبِيُّكَ (سَيِّدُنَا) مُحَمَّدٌ صَلَّى

اللّٰهُ عَلَيْهِ وَاٰلِهٖ وَسَلَّمَ وَنَعُوْذُبِكَ مِنْ شَرِّ مَا اسْتَعَاذَ مِنْهُ نَبِيُّكَ (سَيِّدُنَا)

مُحَمَّدٌ صَلَّى اللّٰهُ عَلَيْهِ وَاٰلِهٖ وَسَلَّمَ وَ اَنْتَ الْمُسْتَعَانُ وَعَلَيْكَ الْبَلَاغُ وَلَا

حَوْلَ وَلَا قُوَّةَ اِلَّا بِاللّٰهِ

O Allāh! Indeed we ask You of all good that Your Prophet (our master) Muḥammad asked You of, and we seek refuge in You from all evil that Your Prophet (our master) Muḥammad sought refuge from. You are the one whose help is sought and You are the one to make it reach (us); there is no might and strength except with Allāh.

Ḥaḍrat Abu Umāma ؓ once said to Rasulullāh ﷺ. You have made innumerable duʿās but we do not remember any of them." Rasulullāh ﷺ replied: "Should I not show you such a comprehensive duʿā which includes these duʿās? Then Rasulullāh ﷺ taught him the above duʿā.[29]

---

28 Faḍāil Durūd
29 Tirmidhi

20

اَللّٰهُمَّ صَلِّ عَلٰى سَيِّدِنَا مُحَمَّدٍ صَلٰوةً تُنْجِيْنَا بِهَا مِنْ جَمِيْعِ الْاَهْوَالِ

وَالْاٰفَاتِ وَتَقْضِيْ لَنَا بِهَا جَمِيْعَ الْحَاجَاتِ وَتُطَهِّرُنَا بِهَا مِنْ جَمِيْعِ

السَّيِّئَاتِ وَتَرْفَعُنَا بِهَا اَعْلَى الدَّرَجَاتِ وَتُبَلِّغُنَا بِهَا اَقْصَى الْغَايَاتِ مِنْ

جَمِيْعِ الْخَيْرَاتِ فِي الْحَيٰوةِ وَبَعْدَ الْمَمَاتِ اِنَّكَ عَلٰى كُلِّ شَيْءٍ قَدِيْرٌ

O Allāh! Confer your blessings upon (our master) Muḥammad, such blessings that will save us from all dangers and misfortunes and that will fulfil for us all our needs, and that will cleanse us from all evil, and that will raise us to high positions, and that will cause us to reach all our desired righteous aims, in this world, and after death. Verily, You have power over all things

This ṣalāt is a means of fulfilling one's needs. The mashāikh have stated from experience that it safeguards one from calamities if it is read seventy times after ṣalātul ʿIsha. Its reading has been tried and tested and found to be beneficial.

وَآخِرُ دَعْوَانَا اَنِ الْحَمْدُ لِلّٰهِ رَبِّ الْعَالَمِيْنَ

And our final prayer is that all praise is due to Allāh, the Lord of worlds.

Reading ṣalawāt abundantly on the day of Jumuʿa

Sayyidunā Abū Hurayra ﷺ narrated that whoever confers the following blessings eighty times before getting up from his place after ʿAṣr prayers on Jumuʿa, eighty years of his sins will be forgiven and he will be granted the reward of eighty years of worship:

$$ اَللّٰهُمَّ صَلِّ عَلٰى مُحَمَّدٍ النَّبِيِّ الْأُمِّيِّ وَعَلٰى اٰلِهٖ وَسَلِّمْ تَسْلِيْمًا $$

O Allāh, confer blessings upon Muḥammad, the unlettered prophet, and upon his family and confer worthy salutations (upon him).

In a narration of Dār Quṭni ﷲ this ṣalāt is up to and including النَّبِيِّ الْأُمِّيِّ. Ḥāfiẓ Irāqi ﷲ has declared this ḥadīth ḥasan (a good chain of transmission). In al-Jāmi al-Saghīr this ḥadīth is narrated by Ḥaḍrat Abu Hurayra ﷺ and has been graded as ḥasan (sound).

Ḥaḍrat Sheikhul Ḥadīth Mawlāna Zakariyya's ﷲ regular routine on the day of Jumuʿa after ʿAsr prayers was to read these ṣalawāt eighty times. He used to also encourage his attendants to do likewise.

There are numerous virtues of doing ṣalawāt in abundance on the blessed day of Jumuʿa. Ḥaḍrat Abu Dardā ﷺ narrates that Rasulullāh ﷺ said, "Confer blessings upon me abundantly on Jumuʿa, for it is a day in which the angels are present. Nobody confers blessings upon me except that his blessings are presented to me as soon as he has conferred them." Abu Dardā ﷺ asked, "O Messenger of Allāh, will this happen after you have passed away too?" The Noble Prophet ﷺ replied, "Verily, Allāh has forbidden the earth from decomposing the bodies of the

Prophets عَلَيْهِمُ السَّلَام. The Prophet of Allāh is alive and granted sustenance."

It is narrated from Rasulullāh ﷺ "Confer blessings upon me abundantly on Jumu'a, for the blessings of my followers are presented to me every Jumu'a." i.e. the ṣalawāt are presented immediately as in the previous ḥadīth.

It has also been narrated on the authority of Ḥaḍrat 'Umar ؓ that the Noble Prophet ﷺ said, "Confer blessings upon me abundantly on the luminous night and the luminous day (the night and day of Jumu'a), for your ṣalawāt are presented to me and I supplicate and seek forgiveness on your behalf."

Ibn Qayyim رَحِمَهُ اللّٰه said, "The virtue of conferring blessings on Jumu'a is because Jumu'a is the leader of all days and the Prophet ﷺ is the leader of all the Prophets عَلَيْهِمُ السَّلَام. Thus, Jumu'a has a strong bond with conferring blessings upon the Noble Prophet ﷺ which no other day has."

For these reasons those who read Ḥizbul A'ẓam regularly should not simply rely on the ṣalawāt contained therein. The preceding virtues should be kept in mind and one should be eager to read ṣalawāt profusely. Whether it be Salāt Ibrāhimiyya (as we read in five times prayers) a hundred times or or the one after 'Asr prayers ṣalāt above or وَ صَلَّ اللّٰهُ عَلَى النَّبِيِّ الأُمِّيِّ (this ṣalāt has been narrated in ḥadīth) five hundred times. Also, the forty ṣalawāt and salām narrated from sound aḥādīth narrated in Faḍāil Durūd should also be read. The reader will be rewarded for ṣalawāt and for reading forty aḥādīth.

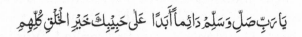

يَا رَبِّ صَلِّ وَسَلِّمْ دَائِمًا أَبَدًا عَلَى حَبِيْبِكَ خَيْرِ الْخَلْقِ كُلِّهِمِ

Day Two

1

بِسْمِ اللهِ الرَّحْمٰنِ الرَّحِيْمِ

اَلْحَمْدُ لِلّٰهِ رَبِّ الْعٰلَمِيْنَ ❋ الرَّحْمٰنِ الرَّحِيْمِ ❋ مٰلِكِ يَوْمِ الدِّيْنِ ❋ اِيَّاكَ نَعْبُدُ وَاِيَّاكَ نَسْتَعِيْنُ ❋ اِهْدِنَا الصِّرَاطَ الْمُسْتَقِيْمَ ❋ صِرَاطَ الَّذِيْنَ أَنْعَمْتَ عَلَيْهِمْ غَيْرِ الْمَغْضُوْبِ عَلَيْهِمْ وَلَا الضَّآلِّيْنَ ❋

2

اَللّٰهُمَّ صَلِّ عَلٰى مُحَمَّدٍ وَّعَلٰى آلِ مُحَمَّدٍ كَمَا صَلَّيْتَ عَلٰى إِبْرَاهِيْمَ وَعَلٰى آلِ إِبْرَاهِيْمَ إِنَّكَ حَمِيْدٌ مَّجِيْدٌ اَللّٰهُمَّ بَارِكْ عَلٰى مُحَمَّدٍ وَّعَلٰى آلِ مُحَمَّدٍ كَمَا بَارَكْتَ عَلٰى إِبْرَاهِيْمَ وَعَلٰى آلِ إِبْرَاهِيْمَ إِنَّكَ حَمِيْدٌ مَّجِيْدٌ

O Allāh! Confer your blessings upon Muḥammad and the family of Muḥammad just as you conferred blessings upon Ibrāhīm and the family of Ibrāhīm. Verily, You are the Praiseworthy, the Majestic. O Allāh, bless Muḥammad and the family of Muḥammad just as you blessed Ibrāhīm and the family of Ibrāhīm. Indeed You are the Praiseworthy, the Majestic.

This ṣalāt is narrated in Bukhāri Sharīf. It is the most authentic and virtuous ṣalāt. Its recital should be done with diligence within the five times prayers and at other times as well. Rasulullāh ﷺ taught this ṣalāt himself and Allāh ﷻ sent Jibril عليه السلام to teach this ṣalāt.[30] The mashāikh have stated that اَللّٰهُمَّ is to call Allāh ﷻ by all his beautiful names at once and حَمِيْدٌ مَّجِيْدٌ are two such blessed names of Allāh ﷻ that all of His attributes are contained therein, whether they be his attributes of beauty or attributes of majesty. Therfore, while reading this ṣalāt the meaning of these names of Allāh ﷻ should be reflected upon. By means of this, the spiritual benefits of the ṣalāt will be great.

3

$$رَبَّنَا آتِنَا فِي الدُّنْيَا حَسَنَةً وَّفِي الْأٰخِرَةِ حَسَنَةً وَّقِنَا عَذَابَ النَّارِ$$

بقرة

O our Lord! Grant us good in this world and good in the life to come and keep us safe from the torment of the Fire

According to aḥādīth of Bukhāri and Muslim, this was the most oft-repeated duʿā of the Prophet ﷺ. In other narrations, he used to make this duʿā during tawaf.

4

$$قُلِ اللّٰهُمَّ مَالِكَ الْمُلْكِ تُؤْتِي الْمُلْكَ مَنْ تَشَاءُ وَتَنْزِعُ الْمُلْكَ مِمَّنْ تَشَاءُ$$

$$وَتُعِزُّ مَنْ تَشَاءُ وَتُذِلُّ مَنْ تَشَاءُ بِيَدِكَ الْخَيْرُ إِنَّكَ عَلٰى كُلِّ شَيْءٍ قَدِيْرٌ$$

---

30 Faḍāil Durūd

۞ تُوْلِجُ الَّيْلَ فِي النَّهَارِ وَتُوْلِجُ النَّهَارَ فِي الَّيْلِ وَتُخْرِجُ الْحَيَّ مِنَ الْمَيِّتِ وَتُخْرِجُ الْمَيِّتَ مِنَ الْحَيِّ وَتَرْزُقُ مَنْ تَشَآءُ بِغَيْرِ حِسَابٍ ۞

آل عمران

Say O Allāh! O Lord of the kingdom! You give kingdom to whom You will, and take kingdom away from whom You will; and You bestow honour on whom You will, and bring disgrace to whom You will. In your hand lies the betterment (of everyone). You are surely powerful over everything. You make the night enter into the day, and make the day enter into the night; and You bring the living out from the dead, and bring the dead out from the living, and You give to whom You will beyond measure.

Rasulullāh ﷺ was ordered to make du'ā in this form. In another narration the Ismul A'ẓam[31] is contained within these verses. When someone calls Allāh ﷻ by this name, du'ās are accepted.

5

رَبِّ هَبْ لِيْ مِنْ لَّدُنْكَ ذُرِّيَّةً طَيِّبَةً ۖ إِنَّكَ سَمِيْعُ الدُّعَآءِ

آل عمران

O my Lord! Grant me by Your own (power) a good progeny. Verily, You are the One who listens to the prayer.

---

31 The greatest name of Allāh

This is the duʿā of Ḥaḍrat Zakariyya ﷺ. He was an old man and there was no possibility of having children. He made this duʿā when he saw out of season fruits with Ḥaḍrat Maryam عَلَيْهَاالسَّلَام.

6

رَبَّنَآ اٰمَنَّا بِمَآ اَنْزَلْتَ وَاتَّبَعْنَا الرَّسُوْلَ فَاكْتُبْنَا مَعَ الشّٰهِدِيْنَ

آل عمران

Our Lord! We have believed in what You have revealed, and we have followed the messenger. So, record us with those who bear witness (to the Truth).

This is the duʿā of Ḥaḍrat ʿĪsā's ﷺ disciples which has been revealed in the Holy Qurān. In one ḥadīth, a long duʿā after ṣalāt has been narrated and the above verse is the end of that duʿā.[32]

7

رَبَّنَا مَا خَلَقْتَ هٰذَا بَاطِلًا سُبْحَانَكَ فَقِنَا عَذَابَ النَّارِ ۞ رَبَّنَآ

اِنَّكَ مَنْ تُدْخِلِ النَّارَ فَقَدْ اَخْزَيْتَهُ وَمَا لِلظّٰلِمِيْنَ مِنْ اَنْصَارٍ

۞ رَبَّنَآ اِنَّنَا سَمِعْنَا مُنَادِيًا يُّنَادِىْ لِلْاِيْمَانِ اَنْ اٰمِنُوْا بِرَبِّكُمْ فَاٰمَنَّا رَبَّنَا

فَاغْفِرْ لَنَا ذُنُوْبَنَا وَكَفِّرْ عَنَّا سَيِّاٰتِنَا وَتَوَفَّنَا مَعَ الْاَبْرَارِ ۞ رَبَّنَا وَاٰتِنَا مَا وَعَدْتَّنَا عَلٰى رُسُلِكَ وَلَا تُخْزِنَا يَوْمَ الْقِيٰمَةِ اِنَّكَ لَا تُخْلِفُ الْمِيْعَادَ

Our Lord, You have not created all this in vain. We proclaim Your purity. So, save us from the punishment of Fire. Our Lord, whomsoever You admit into the Fire, he is disgraced by You indeed, and for the unjust there are no supporters. Our Lord, We heard a herald calling towards Faith: 'Believe in your Lord.' So we believed. Our Lord, forgive us, then, our sins, and write off our evil deeds, and make us die only when we have joined the righteous. Our Lord, give us what You have promised us through Your messengers, and do not put us to disgrace on the Day of Judgement. Surely you do not go back on Your promise.

Ḥaḍrat Abu Hurayra ؓ has narrated that Rasululah ﷺ used to read the last ten verses of sura Āl-'Imrān at night. Ḥaḍrat 'Usmān ؓ has narrated that whoever reads the end of sura Āl-'Imrān at night, he will get the reward of standing in prayer the whole night.[33]

8

رَبِّ اجْعَلْنِيْ مُقِيْمَ الصَّلٰوةِ وَمِنْ ذُرِّيَّتِيْ رَبَّنَا وَتَقَبَّلْ دُعَآءِ ۞ رَبَّنَا اغْفِرْ لِيْ وَلِوَالِدَيَّ وَلِلْمُؤْمِنِيْنَ يَوْمَ يَقُوْمُ الْحِسَابُ ۞

---

33 Ad-dur rul Manthūr

سُوْرَةُ إبراهيم

My Lord! Make me establisher of prayer and also from my progeny.
And Our Lord! Grant my prayer. Our Lord! Forgive me and my
parents and all believers on the day when reckoning shall take place."

This is the du'ā of Ḥaḍrat Ibrāhīm ﷺ. It is one of the du'ās to be
recited whilst sitting before the end of ṣalāt.

9

رَّبِّ ارْحَمْهُمَا كَمَا رَبَّيَانِيْ صَغِيْرًا

سُوْرَةُ بني اسرآئيل / الإسرَاء

My Lord, be merciful to them as they have brought me up in my
childhood.

In this du'ā, Allāh teaches us how to make du'ā for parents. So
du'ā should be made for them with these words

10

رَبَّنَا لَا تَجْعَلْنَا فِتْنَةً لِّلْقَوْمِ الظّٰلِمِيْنَ ۞ وَنَجِّنَا بِرَحْمَتِكَ مِنَ الْقَوْمِ
الْكٰفِرِيْنَ ۞

سُوْرَةُ يُونس

42

Our Lord! Do not make us a victim of the unjust people. And save us, through Your mercy, from the disbelieving people.

Ḥaḍrat Musa ﷻ taught this duʿā to his companions for protection from evil trials and tribulations.

11

اَللّٰهُمَّ صَلِّ وَسَلِّمْ أَشْرَفَ الصَّلٰوةِ وَالتَّسْلِيْمِ عَلٰى حَبِيْبِكَ سَيِّدِنَا وَ

نَبِيِّنَا مُحَمَّدٍ عَبْدِكَ وَرَسُوْلِكَ الَّذِىْ جَعَلْتَ اِتِّبَاعَهُ مُوْجِبًا لِمَحَبَّتِكَ

حَيْثُ قُلْتَ فِىْ حَقِّهِ

﴿قُلْ اِنْ كُنْتُمْ تُحِبُّوْنَ اللهَ فَاتَّبِعُوْنِىْ يُحْبِبْكُمُ اللهُ﴾

آل عمران

O Allāh! Confer the noblest peace and blessings on your beloved, our master and prophet Muḥammad Your slave and messenger the one whose imitation You have made a requirement for (achieving) Your love, as You have declared that " Say (O Prophet): "If you really love Allāh, then follow me, and Allāh shall love you."

Allāh ﷻ has made the imitation of Rasulullāh ﷺ a condition for his love. From this Rasulullāh's ﷺ status and the love of Allāh ﷻ for him above all becomes evident.

12

﴾ رَبِّ اَنِّيْ مَسَّنِيَ الضُّرُّ وَاَنْتَ اَرْحَمُ الرّٰحِمِيْنَ ﴿

سُوْرَةُ الْاَنْبِيَاء

O my Lord! Here I am, afflicted by pain and You are the most merciful of all the merciful.

This is the du'ā of Ḥaḍrat Ayyūb . It is narrated from Ḥaḍrat Imam Jā'far As-Ṣādiq رَحِمَهُ اللّٰه that it is found from experience that it is effective against calamities and sicknesses.

13

﴾ رَبِّ لَا تَذَرْنِيْ فَرْدًا وَّاَنْتَ خَيْرُ الْوَارِثِيْنَ ﴿

سُوْرَةُ الْاَنْبِيَاء

My Lord Do not leave me alone and You are the best of inheritors.

This is the du'ā of Ḥaḍrat Zakariyya عليه السلام. One should ask for children from Allāh ﷻ by means of this du'ā.

14

﴾ لَا اِلٰهَ اِلَّا اَنْتَ سُبْحٰنَكَ اِنِّيْ كُنْتُ مِنَ الظّٰلِمِيْنَ ﴿

سُوْرَةُ الْاَنْبِيَاء

There is no one worthy of worship except You. Pure are You. Indeed, I was among the wrongdoers.

This is the du'ā of Ḥaḍrat Yūnus Bin Matta ﷺ. Rasulullāh ﷺ has said that Allāh has a name and when someone beseeches Him by that name, then whatever du'ā they make it is accepted. Whatever they ask for it is given to them. This is the greatest name of Allāh i.e. al-Ismul A'ẓam. This name is contained in the above verse.

It has been narrated in a Ḥadīth that whoever is sick and reads this du'ā forty times, they will achieve the status of a shahīd. Numerous other virtues of this verse have been narrated. It is a tried and tested formula for alleviating misfortune and calamaties.[34]

15

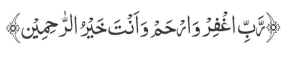

سُوَرَةُ المؤمنون

My Lord! Grant pardon and have mercy, for you are the best of all the merciful.

Rasulullāh ﷺ was ordered to make this du'ā.

---

34 Ad-dur rul Manthūr

16

سُوْرَةُ الفُرقان

Our Lord! Bestow on us from our wives and our offspring the
comfort of our eyes, and make us leaders for those that fear (Allāh).

This du'ā is to make one's family from those who have taqwa
and to achieve for one's self a high level of taqwa.

17

﴿ رَبِّ اِنِّیْ لِمَاۤ اَنْزَلْتَ اِلَیَّ مِنْ خَیْرٍ فَقِیْرٌ ﴾

سُوْرَةُ القَصَص

My Lord! I am in need of whatever good you send down to me.

This is the du'ā of Ḥaḍrat Musa ﷺ. This du'ā is to remove
poverty and being in need (of others).

18

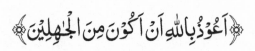

سُوْرَةُ البَقَرَة

I seek refuge with Allāh from being one of the ignorant.

This du'ā is refuge from ignorance and misguidance.

19

﴿رَبَّنَا لَا تُزِغْ قُلُوبَنَا بَعْدَ إِذْ هَدَيْتَنَا وَهَبْ لَنَا مِنْ لَّدُنْكَ

رَحْمَةً ۚ إِنَّكَ أَنْتَ الْوَهَّابُ﴾

سُوْرَةُ آلِ عِمْرَان

*Our Lord, do not let our hearts deviate from the right path after You
have given us guidance, and bestow upon us mercy from Your own
self. Surely, You, and You alone, are the One who bestows in
abundance.*

Ḥaḍrat Umm Salama ﵂ has narrated that Rasulullāh ﷺ used
to read the du'ā يَا مُقَلِّبَ الْقُلُوْبِ ثَبِّتْ قَلْبِيْ عَلٰى دِيْنِكَ abundantly then he
used to read the above du'ā until the end. It is narrated from
Ḥaḍrat 'Āisha ﵂ that she observed that Rasulullāh ﷺ used
to read this du'ā at night.[35]

20

اَللّٰهُمَّ أَنْتَ رَبِّيْ لَا إِلٰهَ إِلَّا أَنْتَ خَلَقْتَنِيْ وَأَنَا عَبْدُكَ وَأَنَا عَلٰى عَهْدِكَ

وَوَعْدِكَ مَا اسْتَطَعْتُ أَعُوْذُ بِكَ مِنْ شَرِّ مَا صَنَعْتُ أَبُوْءُ لَكَ بِنِعْمَتِكَ

---

35 Ad-dur rul Manthūr

47

عَلَيَّ وَ أَبُوءُ بِذَنْبِي فَاغْفِرْ لِي فَإِنَّهُ لَا يَغْفِرُ الذُّنُوبَ إِلَّا أَنْتَ

O Allāh! You are my Lord, there is none worthy of worship but You.
You created me and I am Your slave. I keep Your covenant, and my
pledge to You so far as I am able. I seek refuge in You from the evil of
what I have done. I admit to Your blessings upon me, and I admit to
my misdeeds. Forgive me, For there is none who may forgive sins but
You.

Among the various du'ās for istighfār (seeking forgiveness) this
is the most comprehensive. It is called Sayyidul Istighfār or the
leader of istighfār. Rasulullāh ﷺ has said that whoever read this
with yaqīn during the day and dies before the evening, he will
enter paradise. And whoever reads it with yaqīn in the night
and dies before the morning will be from the people of
paradise.[36]

21

اَللّٰهُمَّ إِنَّا نَسْئَلُكَ مِنْ خَيْرِ مَا سَئَلَكَ مِنْهُ نَبِيُّكَ (سَيِّدُنَا) مُحَمَّدٌ صَلَّى

اللهُ عَلَيْهِ وَالِهِ وَسَلَّمَ وَنَعُوْذُ بِكَ مِنْ شَرِّ مَا اسْتَعَاذَ مِنْهُ نَبِيُّكَ (سَيِّدُنَا)

مُحَمَّدٌ صَلَّى اللهُ عَلَيْهِ وَالِهِ وَسَلَّمَ وَ أَنْتَ الْمُسْتَعَانُ وَعَلَيْكَ الْبَلَاغُ وَلَا

حَوْلَ وَلَا قُوَّةَ إِلَّا بِاللهِ

O Allāh! Indeed, we ask You of all good that Your Prophet (our master) Muḥammad ﷺ asked You of, and we seek refuge in You from all evil that Your Prophet (our master) Muḥammad ﷺ sought refuge from. You are the one whose help is sought and the one to make it reach (us); there is no power and strength except with Allāh.

22

اَللّٰهُمَّ صَلِّ وَسَلِّمْ أَشْرَفَ الصَّلٰوةِ وَالتَّسْلِيْمِ عَلٰى حَبِيْبِكَ سَيِّدِنَا وَنَبِيِّنَا

مُحَمَّدٍ عَبْدِكَ وَرَسُوْلِكَ الَّذِىْ قَرَنْتَ اِسْمَهُ مَعَ اِسْمِكَ حَيْثُ قُلْتَ فِيْ

حَقِّهٖ ۞ وَرَفَعْنَا لَكَ ذِكْرَكَ ۞

سُوْرَةُ الشَّرْح

O Allāh confer the noblest peace and blessings on your beloved, our master and prophet Muḥammad, Your slave and messenger the one whose name you have attached to Your own name as You have declared "And We elevated your remembrance."

The name of Allāh being exalted is obvious. Any other names that are attached to it are also exalted. That is why the kalima of Islam, athān, Iqāma, five times ṣalāt and khutba all have the praises of Allāh and ṣalāt on the Prophet ﷺ along with it.

وَآخِرُ دَعْوَانَا أَنِ الْحَمْدُ لِلّٰهِ رَبِّ الْعَالَمِيْنَ

Mukhtaṣarul Ḥizbul Aʾẓam – Day Two

Day Three

1

بِسْمِ اللهِ الرَّحْمٰنِ الرَّحِيْمِ

اَلْحَمْدُ لِلّٰهِ رَبِّ الْعٰلَمِيْنَ ۞ الرَّحْمٰنِ الرَّحِيْمِ ۞ مٰلِكِ يَوْمِ الدِّيْنِ ۞ إِيَّاكَ نَعْبُدُ وَإِيَّاكَ نَسْتَعِيْنُ ۞ اِهْدِنَا الصِّرَاطَ الْمُسْتَقِيْمَ ۞ صِرَاطَ الَّذِيْنَ أَنْعَمْتَ عَلَيْهِمْ غَيْرِ الْمَغْضُوْبِ عَلَيْهِمْ وَلَا الضَّالِّيْنَ ۞

2

اَللّٰهُمَّ صَلِّ وَسَلِّمْ أَشْرَفَ الصَّلٰوةِ وَالتَّسْلِيْمِ عَلٰى حَبِيْبِكَ سَيِّدِنَا وَنَبِيِّنَا مُحَمَّدٍ عَبْدِكَ وَرَسُوْلِكَ الَّذِىْ أَكْرَمْتَهُ بِأَكْمَلِ الْخُلُقِ حَيْثُ قُلْتَ فِىْ حَقِّهِ

﴿ وَإِنَّكَ لَعَلٰى خُلُقٍ عَظِيْمٍ ﴾

سُوْرَةُ الْقَلَم

51

O Allāh! Confer the noblest peace and blessings on your beloved, our master and prophet Muḥammad Your slave and messenger the one who You have honoured with the most exalted character as You have declared that "And verily, you are on an exalted (standard of) charcater".

Allāh ﷻ has declared regarding Rasulullāh ﷺ that *and verily, you are on an exalted (standard of) character*. One should reflect on how exalted a being must be that Allāh ﷻ himself has referred to him as being exalted.

3

اَللّٰهُمَّ لَكَ الْحَمْدُ كَمَاۤ أَنْتَ أَهْلُهٗ فَصَلِّ وَسَلِّمْ عَلٰى (سَيِّدِنَا) لِمُحَمَّدٍ كَمَاۤ أَنْتَ أَهْلُهٗ فَافْعَلْ بِنَا مَاۤ أَنْتَ أَهْلُهٗ فَإِنَّكَ أَهْلُ التَّقْوٰى وَأَهْلُ الْمَغْفِرَةِ

O Allāh! All praise is for you as befitting (your majesty) and confer peace and blessings upon (our master) Muḥammad as befitting (your majesty) and deal with us in a manner befitting (Your majesty) for indeed You are worthy to be feared, and worthy to forgive.

'Allama ibn Mushtahir رَحِمَهُ اللّٰه said that whoever wants to praise Allāh ﷻ in the most virtuous way that he could ever be praised by any creation, from the first or the last of the creation, or from the angels that are near to Allāh ﷻ, or from anyone from those who are on the earth or those in the heavens. And if one wants to read ṣalāt on the Holy Prophet ﷺ which is the most virtuous, then he should read as above and similarly if he wants to make duʿā to Allāh ﷻ in the most virtuous form then he should read the same as duʿā.[37]

4

رَبِّ اَوْزِعْنِیْٓ اَنْ اَشْکُرَ نِعْمَتَکَ الَّتِیْٓ اَنْعَمْتَ عَلَیَّ وَعَلٰی وَالِدَیَّ وَاَنْ اَعْمَلَ صَالِحًا تَرْضٰىهُ وَاَصْلِحْ لِیْ فِیْ ذُرِّیَّتِیْ اِنِّیْ تُبْتُ اِلَیْکَ وَاِنِّیْ مِنَ الْمُسْلِمِیْنَ ۞

سُوْرَۃُ الْاَحْقاف

My Lord! Grant me that I offer gratitude for the favour You have bestowed upon me and upon my parents, and that I do righteous deeds that You like. And set righteousness, for my sake, in my progeny. Of course, I repent to you, and truly I am one of those who submit to You.

This Qurānic verse was revealed regarding Ḥaḍrat Abu Bakr As-Ṣiddīq ﷺ. He made a duʿā which Allāh ﷻ has mentioned and accepted in such a way that his parents, children and brothers all became Muslim. Ḥaḍrat Abu Muʿshir complained to Ḥaḍrat Talḥa bin Musrif رحمه الله about the disobedience of his son. He advised him to seek help by means of this verse.[38] For seeking *hidaya* for kith and kin then this duʿā should be made.

---

37 Faḍāil Durūd
38 Durr Manthūr

5

رَبَّنَا اغْفِرْ لَنَا وَلِإِخْوَانِنَا الَّذِينَ سَبَقُونَا بِالْإِيمَانِ وَلَا تَجْعَلْ فِي قُلُوبِنَا غِلًّا

لِلَّذِينَ آمَنُوا رَبَّنَا إِنَّكَ رَؤُوفٌ رَّحِيمٌ

سُوْرَةُ آل عِمرَان

Our Lord! Forgive us and those of our brothers who preceded us in faith, and do not place in our hearts any rancor against those who believe; Surely, Our Lord, you are Very-Kind, Very-Merciful.

Through this duʿā forgiveness is sought for those believers who have passed away and to remember them positively. It is narrated from Ḥaḍrat ʿĀisha رضي الله عنها that she said that Muslims are ordered to make duʿā for the Ṣaḥāba of the Prophet ﷺ, but now people disobey this order and criticise the Ṣaḥāba. Then she recited the above verse.[39]

6

اللَّهُمَّ إِنِّي أَسْأَلُكَ بِأَنِّي أَشْهَدُ أَنَّكَ أَنْتَ اللهُ لَا إِلَهَ إِلَّا أَنْتَ الْأَحَدُ

الصَّمَدُ الَّذِي لَمْ يَلِدْ وَلَمْ يُولَدْ وَلَمْ يَكُنْ لَّهُ كُفُوًا أَحَدٌ

O Allāh! Indeed, I ask you (with these words) that indeed I bear witness that there is no one worthy of worship except You, the Self-

---

39 Durre Manthūr

Sufficient master, whom all creatures need, He begets not nor was He begotten, and there is none equal to Him.

In the aḥādīth this is referred to as al-Ismul Aʿẓam or the great name of Allāh ﷻ that when you make duʿā by the same, the duʿā is accepted by Allāh ﷻ.[40]

7

$$اللّٰهُمَّ إِنِّيْ أَسْأَلُكَ الْعَفْوَ وَالْعَافِيَةَ فِيْ دِيْنِيْ وَدُنْيَايَ وَأَهْلِيْ وَمَالِيْ$$

O Allāh! I seek your forgiveness and well-being in my my religion, my worldly life, my family and my wealth.

Duʿā for well-being is the most beloved duʿā to Allāh ﷻ because within it one expresses servitude. In a ḥadīth it is mentioned that after imān the greatest and best thing is well-being.[41]

8

$$يَا حَيُّ يَا قَيُّوْمُ بِرَحْمَتِكَ أَسْتَغِيْثُ أَصْلِحْ لِيْ شَأْنِيْ كُلَّهُ وَلَا تَكِلْنِيْ إِلٰى نَفْسِيْ طَرْفَةَ عَيْنٍ$$

O Ever Living! O Self-Subsisting and Supporter of all! By Your mercy I seek assistance. Rectify for me all my affairs and do not leave me to myself, even for the blink of an eye.

---

40 The Four Sunan, Musnad Aḥmad and Ibn Ḥibban
41 Abu Dawūd, Nasāi, etc

This du'ā also contains the Ismul A'ẓam. Rasulullāh ﷺ used to make this du'ā frequently. He also ordered Ḥaḍrat Fātima رَضِيَ اللهُ عَنْهَا to read this every morning and evening.[42]

9

اَللّٰهُمَّ إِنِّيْ أَسْأَلُكَ صِحَّةً فِيْ إِيْمَانٍ وَإِيْمَانًا فِيْ حُسْنِ خُلُقٍ وَنَّجَاحًا يَتْبَعُهُ

فَلَاحٌ وَّرَحْمَةً مِّنْكَ وَعَافِيَةً وَّمَغْفِرَةً مِّنْكَ وَرِضْوَانًا

O Allāh! I ask You for soundness of belief; for a faith which leads to good conduct; for a success which results in eternal felicity; for mercy, health and forgiveness from You, and for Your pleasure.

Ḥaḍrat Rasulullāh ﷺ taught this du'ā to Salmān Fārsi ؓ and called these *Kalimāt ur Rahmān* or the *words of the Most Merciful*. The Prophet ﷺ advised to make this du'ā day and night and to do so towards Allāh ﷻ with yearning.[43]

10

اَللّٰهُمَّ اغْفِرْ لِيْ ذَنْبِيْ وَوَسِّعْ لِيْ فِيْ دَارِيْ وَبَارِكْ لِيْ فِيْ رِزْقِيْ

O Allāh! Forgive my sins and widen my home and grant baraka in my rizq.

---

42 Nasāi and Ḥākim
43 Mu'jamul Awsat

This is a comprehensive duʿā for forgiveness and baraka. It is sunna to read this during wuḍu. [44]

11

اَللّٰهُمَّ اجْعَلْ فِيْ قَلْبِيْ نُوْرًا وَّفِيْ بَصَرِيْ نُوْرًا وَّفِيْ سَمْعِيْ نُوْرًا وَّعَنْ يَمِيْنِيْ نُوْرًا وَّعَنْ شِمَالِيْ نُوْرًا وَّمِنْ خَلْفِيْ نُوْرًا وَّمِنْ أَمَامِيْ نُوْرًا وَّاجْعَلْ مِنْ فَوْقِيْ نُوْرًا وَّمِنْ تَحْتِيْ نُوْرًا اَللّٰهُمَّ أَعْطِنِيْ نُوْرًا وَّاجْعَلْ لِيْ نُوْرًا وَّفِيْ عَصَبِيْ نُوْرًا وَّفِيْ لَحْمِيْ نُوْرًا وَّفِيْ دَمِيْ نُوْرًا وَّفِيْ شَعْرِيْ نُوْرًا وَّفِيْ بَشَرِيْ نُوْرًا وَّفِيْ لِسَانِيْ نُوْرًا وَّاجْعَلْ فِيْ نَفْسِيْ نُوْرًا وَّأَعْظِمْ لِيْ نُوْرًا وَّاجْعَلْنِيْ نُوْرًا

O Allāh! Place nūr in my heart, nūr on my tongue, nūr in my hearing, nūr in my sight, nūr behind me, nūr in front of me, nūr on my right, nūr on my left, nūr above me and nūr below me; place nūr in my sinew, in my flesh, in my blood, in my hair and in my skin; place nūr in my soul and make nūr abundant for me; make me nūr and grant me nūr.

It is sunna to recite this *duʿā* while going to the *masjid* or at the time of *tahajjud*. The nūr (light) referred to here is hidāya (true guidance) and elucidation of the truth which is connected to every part of the body. For example, seeing the truth, listening to the truth, thinking about the truth etc... and to stay away from all misguidance because all bāṭil (falsehood) is darkness and on

---

44 Nasāi and Ibn Sunni

the Day of Judgement this spiritual light will act as an actual light. The anwār (plural of nūr) of the perfect auliyā (friends of Allāh) can be perceived by people blessed with spiritual insight.[45]

12

اَللّٰهُمَّ صَلِّ وَسَلِّمْ وَ اَشْرَفَ الصَّلوةِ وَ التَّسْلِيمِ عَلٰى حَبِيْبِكَ سَيِّدِنَا وَ

نَبِيِّنَا مُحَمَّدٍ عَبْدِكَ وَ رَسُوْلِكَ الَّذِيْ جَعَلْتَهُ نُوْرًا اَحَيْثُ قُلْتَ

﴿ قَدْ جَآءَكُمْ مِّنَ اللّٰهِ نُوْرٌ وَّ كِتٰبٌ مُّبِيْنٌ ﴾

سُوْرَةُ الْمَائِدة

O Allāh! Confer the noblest peace and blessings on your beloved, our master and prophet Muḥammad Your slave and messenger the one who You have made a nūr (light) "There has come to you, from Allāh, a Light and a clear Book".

From the above verse it becomes apparent that Rasulullāh the master of humanity ﷺ is nūr.[46]

---

45 Bukhārī & Muslim

46 Translator's note: The author's statement when translated is ambiguous. However, the following quote will shed light on what he intended. Mawlāna 'Allāma Muḥammad Sarfaraz Khan Safdar رَحْمَةُاللّٰه writes in his book entitled Tanqīd Matīn 84-85: "It is our belief and research that the leader of all messengers and Seal of the prophets, Sayyiduna Muḥammad (Allāh bless him and give him peace) is bashar (human) as well as nūr; as per his genus and person he is bashar (human), but as per his attribute and guidance he is nūr (light). Due to him, the dark world experienced light, the darkness of kufr and shirk was dispersed and the surface of earth was lit with the rays of imān and tawḥid. Those who were wandering in the darkness of carnal desires and lusts and were falling in the deep pits of disputes and contentions started marching ahead on the bright path of peace and guidance. None of the Muslims can deny this reality. But, if he is considered nūr in a sense that, Allāh forbid – he is denied to be bashar and

13

$$اَللّٰهُمَّ لَاتَجْعَلْ مُصِيبَتَنَا فِيْ دِيْنِنَا وَلَاتَجْعَلِ الدُّنْيَا أَكْبَرَ هَمِّنَا وَلَامَبْلَغَ عِلْمِنَا وَلَاتُسَلِّطْ عَلَيْنَا مَنْ لَايَرْحَمُنَا$$

O Allāh! Place not our calamaties in our religion, and let not this world be our biggest concern, nor the extent of our knowledge. And do not appoint over us one who has no mercy on us.[47]

14

$$رَبِّ أَعْطِ نَفْسِيْ تَقْوَاهَا وَزَكِّهَا أَنْتَ خَيْرُ مَنْ زَكَّاهَا أَنْتَ وَلِيُّهَا وَ مَوْلَاهَا$$

O my Lord! Grant my inner-self its piety, purify it because You are the best of those who can purify it and You are its guardian and master.

Ḥaḍrat 'Āisha رَضِيَ اللهُ عَنْهَا heard this du'ā from Rasulullāh ﷺ while he was in sajda.[48] This is a masnūn du'ā for the purification of the soul and attainment of taqwa.

---

human being all together, then we will oppose it tooth and nail as it is against the nusus (sources of Islam i.e. Qurān and Sunnat)." (English translation of Nūr & Bashar, Ml. Fayyaz A. K. Swati, 1411AH)
47 Ḥisn Ḥasīn
48 Musnad Aḥmad

15

اَللّٰهُمَّ حَاسِبْنِيْ حِسَابًا يَّسِيْرًا

O Allāh! Grant me an easy reckoning.

This is a very important du'ā. The attainment of salvation will be for those whose ḥisāb (reckoning) will be easy and know that the ḥisāb is a reality.[49]

16

اَللّٰهُمَّ أَعِنِّيْ عَلٰى ذِكْرِكَ وَشُكْرِكَ وَحُسْنِ عِبَادَتِكَ

O Allāh! Help me to remember You, give thanks to You and to worship You well.

Nabi ﷺ taught this du'ā to Muadh ؓ and used to read it after ṣalāt.[50]

17

اَللّٰهُمَّ أَصْلِحْ لِيْ دِيْنِيَ الَّذِيْ هُوَ عِصْمَةُ أَمْرِيْ وَ أَصْلِحْ لِيْ دُنْيَايَ الَّتِيْ

فِيْهَا مَعَاشِيْ وَ أَصْلِحْ لِيْ اٰخِرَتِيَ الَّتِيْ فِيْهَا مَعَادِيْ

---

49 Mustadrak Ḥākim
50 Abu Dawūd, Nasāi, etc

O Allāh! Put right for me my dīn in which lies the protection of my affairs and put right for me this world in which lies my livelihood and put right for me the next world in which is my future.

This is a comprehensive prophetic du'ā for wellbeing, progress and success in this world and the hereafter.[51]

18

رَبِّ اغْفِرْ وَارْحَمْ إِنَّكَ أَنْتَ الْأَعَزُّ الْأَكْرَمُ

O Lord! Forgive and have mercy (upon us), verily You are the Mightiest and Noblest

This is a masnūn du'ā.[52]

19

﴿ قَالَ رَبِّ نَجِّنِيْ مِنَ الْقَوْمِ الظَّالِمِيْنَ ﴾

سُوْرَةُ الْقَصَص

O my Lord! Save me from the wrong doers.

This is the du'ā of Ḥaḍrat Musa ﷺ for salvation from oppressors (wrong doers).

---

51 Muslim Sharīf
52 Muṣannaf Ibn Abi Shayba

20

﴿ رَبِّ انْصُرْنِيْ عَلَى الْقَوْمِ الْمُفْسِدِيْنَ ﴾

سُوْرَةُ الْعَنكبوت

My Lord! Help me against the people who make mischief.

This is the du'ā of Ḥaḍrat Lūṭ ﷺ for salvation from the corrupters and oppressors.

21

﴿ رَبِّ إِنِّيْ ظَلَمْتُ نَفْسِيْ فَاغْفِرْ لِيْ ﴾

سُوْرَةُ الْقَصَص

O my Lord! I have wronged myself, so forgive me

This is a comprehensive and concise istighfār.

22

اَللّٰهُمَّ إِنَّا نَسْئَلُكَ مِنْ خَيْرِ مَا سَئَلَكَ مِنْهُ نَبِيُّكَ (سَيِّدُنَا)

مُحَمَّدٌ صَلَّى اللهُ عَلَيْهِ وَاٰلِهٖ وَسَلَّمَ وَنَعُوْذُبِكَ مِنْ شَرِّ مَا اسْتَعَاذَ مِنْهُ نَبِيُّكَ

(سَيِّدُنَا) مُحَمَّدٌ صَلَّى اللهُ عَلَيْهِ وَاٰلِهٖ وَسَلَّمَ وَ أَنْتَ الْمُسْتَعَانُ وَعَلَيْكَ

$$ اَلْبَلَاغُ وَلَا حَوْلَ وَلَا قُوَّةَ إِلَّا بِاللهِ $$

23

$$ اَللّٰهُمَّ صَلِّ وَسَلِّمْ أَشْرَفَ الصَّلٰوةِ وَالتَّسْلِيْمِ عَلٰى حَبِيْبِكَ سَيِّدِنَا وَ $$

$$ نَبِيِّنَا مُحَمَّدٍ عَبْدِكَ وَرَسُوْلِكَ الَّذِىْ قَالَ عَنْ نَفْسِهِ ﴿ أَنَا سَيِّدُ وُلْدِ اٰدَمَ $$

$$ وَلَا فَخْرَ ﴾ $$

O Allāh confer the noblest peace and blessings on your beloved, our master and prophet Muḥammad Your slave and messenger, the one who said about himself "I am the sayyid of the children of Ādam عليه السلام and that is not a matter of (personal pride)".

The ḥadīth[53] quoted in this ṣalāt establishes that Rasulullāh ﷺ is the *sayyid* (leader and master) of all the children of Ḥaḍrat Ādam عليه السلام.

$$ وَاٰخِرُ دَعْوَانَا أَنِ الْحَمْدُ لِلّٰهِ رَبِّ الْعَالَمِيْنَ $$

---

53 Muslim Sharīf

Day Four

1

بِسْمِ اللهِ الرَّحْمٰنِ الرَّحِيْمِ

اَلْحَمْدُ لِلّٰهِ رَبِّ الْعٰلَمِيْنَ ۞ الرَّحْمٰنِ الرَّحِيْمِ ۞ مٰلِكِ يَوْمِ الدِّيْنِ ۞ إِيَّاكَ نَعْبُدُ وَإِيَّاكَ نَسْتَعِيْنُ ۞ اِهْدِنَا الصِّرَاطَ الْمُسْتَقِيْمَ ۞ صِرَاطَ الَّذِيْنَ أَنْعَمْتَ عَلَيْهِمْ غَيْرِ الْمَغْضُوْبِ عَلَيْهِمْ وَلَا الضَّآلِّيْنَ ۞

2

اَللّٰهُمَّ صَلِّ وَسَلِّمْ أَشْرَفَ الصَّلٰوةِ وَالتَّسْلِيْمِ عَلٰى حَبِيْبِكَ سَيِّدِنَا وَ نَبِيِّنَا مُحَمَّدٍ عَبْدِكَ وَرَسُوْلِكَ صَاحِبِ الْمَقَامِ الْمَحْمُوْدِ الَّذِيْ قُلْتَ فِيْ حَقِّهِ ﴿ عَسٰى أَنْ يَّبْعَثَكَ رَبُّكَ مَقَامًا مَّحْمُوْدًا ﴾

سُوْرَةُ الْإِسْرَاء

O Allāh ! Confer the noblest peace and blessings on your beloved, our master and prophet Muḥammad Your slave and messenger the owner of the Maqām Maḥmūd as You have declared that "It is very likely that your Lord will place you at Maqām Maḥmūd".

The *Maqām Maḥmūd* (or the Praised Station) is a place where a seat will be placed for Rasulullāh ﷺ on the right of the throne of Allāh ﷻ on the day of Judgement. When he will be seated his appearance will grace the occasion. Rasulullāh ﷺ will be dressed in two green garments of Paradise. The Banner of Praise shall be in the Prophet's ﷺ hand. All of humanity, the first and the last will be envious of this rank. This shall be the moment of the Great Intercession (of our Prophet ﷺ), by means of which all creation, even the Prophets ﷺ shall derive benefit.

3

اَللّٰهُمَّ اِنَّكَ تَعْلَمُ سِرِّىْ وَ عَلَانِيَتِيْ فَاقْبَلْ مَعْذِرَتِيْ وَتَعْلَمُ

حَاجَتِيْ فَأَعْطِنِيْ سُؤْلِيْ وَتَعْلَمُ مَا فِيْ نَفْسِيْ فَاغْفِرْ لِيْ ذَنْبِيْ اَللّٰهُمَّ اِنِّيْ

أَسْأَلُكَ اِيْمَانًا يُّبَاشِرُ قَلْبِيْ وَيَقِيْنًا صَادِقًا حَتّٰى أَعْلَمُ أَنَّهُ لَا يُصِيْبُنِيْ اِلَّا مَا

كَتَبْتَ لِيْ وَرِضًا بِمَا قَسَمْتَ لِيْ

O Allāh! Indeed You know that which is secret and that which is manifest in me; so accept my apology, You are aware of my need; so grant my petition. You know that which is in my mind, so forgive me my sins. O Allāh! Indeed I beg of You a faith which will engage my heart in firm conviction, so that I may realise that nothing will befall me save what You have prescribed for me, a feeling of satisfaction with that You have alloted unto me.

It is narrated from Ḥaḍrat ʿĀisha رضي الله عنها that she heard Rasulullāh ﷺ saying that when Ādam عليه السلام came down to Earth, he went to the Holy Ka'ba and prayed two raka'ats of ṣalāt and then Allāh ﷻ placed the above du'ā in his heart and he was told that whoever makes this du'ā, I will accept their du'ā and I will suffice for them in regards to their important matters.

4

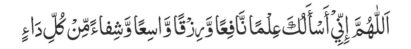

O Allāh! I seek from You beneficial knowledge, ample sustenance and cure from all ailments

After drinking zamzam du'ās are accepted by Allāh ﷻ. This Du'ā is masnoon at that time.[54] It is a very comprehensive du'ā that should be made always.

5

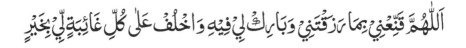

O Allāh! Make me content upon what (blessings) You have granted me and bless me in it; and be the Best Protector (and Guardian) for me (in my absence) of whatever is hidden from me.

This is a marvellous du'ā for contentment and blessings in rizq.[55]

---

54 Mustadrak Ḥākim
55 Mustadrak Ḥākim

6

اَللّٰهُمَّ اهْدِنِيْ بِالْهُدٰى وَنَقِّنِيْ بِالتَّقْوٰى وَاغْفِرْ لِيْ فِي الْاٰخِرَةِ وَالْأُوْلٰى

O Allāh! Guide me with true guidance and purify me by blessing me with taqwa and forgive me in the hereafter and in this world.

This is such an important du'ā that it is narrated that it should be read on the day of ʿArafāt.[56]

7

اللّٰهُمَّ حَبِّبْ إِلَيْنَا الْإِيْمَانَ وَزَيِّنْهُ فِيْ قُلُوْبِنَا وَ كَرِّهْ إِلَيْنَا الْكُفْرَ وَالْفُسُوْقَ

وَالْعِصْيَانَ وَاجْعَلْنَا مِنَ الرَّاشِدِيْنَ

O Allāh! Make imān beloved to us and beautify it in our hearts and make hateful to us disbelief, defiance and disobedience and make us of the rightly guided.

This du'ā is narrated in aḥādīth for imān to permeate the depths of our heart and create an aversion for kufr and all other sins.[57]

---

56 Muṣannaf Ibn Abi Shayba
57 Musnad Aḥmad

8

اَللّٰهُمَّ تَوَفَّنَا مُسْلِمِيْنَ وَ أَلْحِقْنَا بِالصَّالِحِيْنَ غَيْرَ خَزَايَا وَلَا مَفْتُوْنِيْنَ

O Allāh! Let us die as Muslims and make us meet the saliḥīn (righteous) without being disgraced or tried.

This is a special du'ā for death with imān.[58]

9

اَللّٰهُمَّ لَا سَهْلَ إِلَّا مَا جَعَلْتَهُ سَهْلًا وَ أَنْتَ تَجْعَلُ الْحَزَنَ سَهْلًا إِذَا شِئْتَ

O Allāh! There is nothing easy except what You make easy, and You make the difficult easy if it be Your Will.

This is a du'ā narrated from Rasulullāh ﷺ for making difficulties easy.[59]

10

لَا إِلٰهَ إِلَّا اللهُ الْحَلِيْمُ الْكَرِيْمُ سُبْحَانَ اللهِ رَبِّ الْعَرْشِ الْعَظِيْمِ الْحَمْدُ

لِلّٰهِ رَبِّ الْعَالَمِيْنَ أَسْأَلُكَ مُوْجِبَاتِ رَحْمَتِكَ وَ عَزَائِمَ مَغْفِرَتِكَ وَ

الْغَنِيْمَةَ مِنْ كُلِّ بِرٍّ وَّ السَّلَامَةَ مِنْ كُلِّ إِثْمٍ لَا تَدَعْ لِيْ ذَنْبًا إِلَّا غَفَرْتَهُ وَ

---

58 Musnad Aḥmad
59 Ibn Ḥibban & Ibn Sunni

لَاهَمَّا إِلَّا فَرَّجْتَهُ وَلَا كَرْبًا إِلَّا نَفَّسْتَهُ وَلَا ضُرًّا إِلَّا كَشَفْتَهُ وَلَا حَاجَةً

هِيَ لَكَ رِضًا إِلَّا قَضَيْتَهَا يَآ أَرْحَمَ الرَّاحِمِيْنَ

*There is no one worthy of worship but Allāh the Clement and Wise.
There is no one worthy of worship but Allāh the High and Mighty.
Glory be to Allāh, Lord of the Tremendous Throne. All praise is to
Allāh, Lord of the worlds. I ask you (O Allāh) everything that leads
to your mercy, and your tremendous forgiveness, enrichment in all
good, and freedom from all sin. Do not leave a sin of mine (O Allāh),
except that you forgive it, nor any worry except that you create a way
out from it, nor any distress except that you dispel it, nor any harm
except you remove it, nor any need in which there is your good
pleasure except that you fulfill it, O Most Merciful!*

This is the masnūn du'ā for Ṣalātul Ḥajāt or prayer of need.[60]
Experience has shown that by means of this, the needs are
fulfilled. The slave of Allāh ﷻ is continuously in need of Him.

11

اَللّٰهُمَّ صَلِّ وَسَلِّمْ أَشْرَفَ الصَّلٰوةِ وَالتَّسْلِيْمِ عَلٰى حَبِيْبِكَ سَيِّدِنَا وَ

نَبِيِّنَا مُحَمَّدٍ عَبْدِكَ وَرَسُوْلِكَ صَاحِبِ الْحَوْضِ الْمَوْرُوْدِ الَّذِىْ قُلْتَ فِيْ

حَقِّهِ

$$﴿إِنَّا أَعْطَيْنَاكَ الْكَوْثَرَ﴾$$

*O Allāh! Confer the noblest peace and blessings on your beloved,
our master and prophet Muḥammad Your slave and messenger the
owner of the the frequented pond as You have declared that "(O
Prophet,) surely We have given to you al-Kawthar."*

It is narrated in a ḥadīth from Rasulullāh ﷺ that the pond of
Kawthar is in fact a river of Paradise that my Lord has promised
me and it has much goodness in it.

12

$$اَللّٰهُمَّ رَحْمَتَكَ أَرْجُو فَلَا تَكِلْنِي إِلَى نَفْسِي طَرْفَةَ عَيْنٍ وَأَصْلِحْ شَأْنِي كُلَّهُ$$

$$لَا إِلٰهَ إِلَّا أَنْتَ يَا حَيُّ يَا قَيُّومُ بِرَحْمَتِكَ أَسْتَغِيثُ$$

*O Allāh! I hope for Your mercy, do not leave me for even the
duration of an eye blink (duration) and correct my total condition.
Besides You there is none worthy of worship. O Alive and everlasting
One, I beseech You by Your mercy.*

This is a Prophetic duʿā for the removal of all grief and
worry.[61]

---

[61] Abu Dawūd & Tabarāni

71

13

اَللّٰهُمَّ اكْفِنِيْ بِحَلَالِكَ عَنْ حَرَامِكَ وَأَغْنِنِيْ بِفَضْلِكَ عَمَّنْ سِوَاكَ

O Allāh! Save me from ḥarām and make the ḥalāl sufficient and by your grace, make me independent from others.

This is a duʿā for the fulfilment of debts that the Prophet ﷺ taught Ḥaḍrat ʿAli ؓ and he said even if there is a debt equal to that of the mountain of Uḥud, it will be fulfilled.[62]

14

اَللّٰهُمَّ فَارِجَ الْهَمِّ كَاشِفَ الْغَمِّ مُجِيْبَ دَعْوَةِ الْمُضْطَرِّيْنَ رَحْمَانَ الدُّنْيَا وَالْآخِرَةِ وَرَحِيْمَهُمَا أَنْتَ تَرْحَمُنِيْ فَارْحَمْنِيْ بِرَحْمَةٍ تُغْنِيْنِيْ بِهَا عَنْ رَحْمَةِ مَنْ سِوَاكَ

O Allāh! O remover of worry, reliever from grief, the one who responds to the prayers of the distressed ones and the Beneficent and the Merciful in this world and the hereafter. You are merciful to me so have such mercy upon me due to which I dispense with the mercy of any one other than You.

---

[62] Tirmidhi

72

This is also a du'ā for the fulfilment of debts and dispelling of worries and grief.[63]

15

بَّنَآ إِنَّنَآ آمَنَّا فَاغْفِرْ لَنَا ذُنُوْبَنَا وَقِنَا عَذَابَ النَّارِ وَلَا حَوْلَ وَلَاقُوَّةَ إِلَّا

بِاللهِ الْعَلِيِّ الْعَظِيْمِ

Our Lord! We have indeed believed, so forgive us our sins and save us from the punishment of the Fire. And (there is) no power and no strength except from Allāh, the Most High, the Most Great

16

اَللّٰهُمَّ مُصَرِّفَ الْقُلُوْبِ صَرِّفْ قُلُوْبَنَا إِلٰى طَاعَتِكَ

O Allāh! The one who turns the hearts, turn our hearts towards your obedience.

This is a du'ā for the spiritual wellbeing of the heart. Most definitely only Allāh ﷻ controls the hearts.[64]

---

63 Mustadrak Ḥākim
64 Muslim & Nasāi

17

اَللّٰهُمَّ إِنِّيْ أَسْأَلُكَ الْهُدٰى وَالتُّقٰى وَالْعَفَافَ وَالْغِنٰى

O Allāh! Indeed I ask of You, guidance, piety and chastity and to be free of depending on anyone (except You)

A comprehensive masnūn duʿā for dīn and dunya.[65]

18

اَللّٰهُمَّ إِنِّيْ أَعُوْذُبِكَ مِنَ الشِّقَاقِ وَالنِّفَاقِ وَسُوْءِ الْأَخْلَاقِ

O Allāh! I take your refuge from quarrelling, hypocrisy and bad manners.

A beautiful duʿā for protection from the snares of nafs and shaytān.[66]

19

اللّٰهُمَّ مَغْفِرَتُكَ أَوْسَعُ مِنْ ذُنُوْبِيْ وَرَحْمَتُكَ أَرْجٰى عِنْدِيْ مِنْ عَمَلِيْ

O Allāh! Your forgiveness is greater than my sins and my hope in Your mercy is greater to me than my actions.

---

65 Muslim, Tirmidhi & Ibn Māja
66 Abu Dawūd & Nasāi,

Ḥaḍrat Jābir ؓ narrates that once a man came into the prescence of Rasulullāh ﷺ. And he said وَا ذُنُوْبَاه, وَا ذُنُوْبَاه (O my sins, O my sins) [67] two or three times. Rasulullāh ﷺ said to him to recite the above du'ā. The man said this and the Prophet ﷺ said to him, "Say it again." The man repeated it then the Prophet said to him, "Say it again." The man did it and the Prophet ﷺ said to him, "Arise for, indeed, Allāh has forgiven you." [68]

20

$$رَبَّنَآ إِنَّنَآ آمَنَّا فَاغْفِرْ لَنَا ذُنُوْبَنَا وَقِنَا عَذَابَ النَّارِ$$

سُوْرَةُ آل عِمْرَان

O our Lord. Verily, we have believed. So, forgive us our sins and save us from the torment of the Hellfire.

21

$$اَللّٰهُمَّ إِنَّا نَسْئَلُكَ مِنْ خَيْرِ مَا سَاَلَكَ مِنْهُ نَبِيُّكَ (سَيِّدُنَا) مُحَمَّدٌ صَلَّى$$

$$اللهُ تَعَالَى عَلَيْهِ وَالِهِ وَسَلَّمَ وَنَعُوْذُ بِكَ مِنْ شَرِّ مَا اسْتَعَاذَ مِنْهُ نَبِيُّكَ$$

$$(سَيِّدُنَا) مُحَمَّدٌ صَلَّى اللهُ تَعَالَى عَلَيْهِ وَالِهِ وَسَلَّمَ اَنْتَ الْمُسْتَعَانُ وَعَلَيْكَ$$

$$الْبَلَاغُ وَلَا حَوْلَ وَلَا قُوَّةَ إِلَّا بِاللهِ$$

O Allāh! Indeed we ask You of all good that Your Prophet (our master) Muḥammad ﷺ asked You of, and we seek refuge in You from

---

67 The man was overcome and saddened by his state.
68 Mustadrak Ḥākim

all evil that Your Prophet (our master) Muḥammad ﷺ sought refuge from. You are the one whose help is sought and the one to make it reach (us); there is no power and strength except with Allāh.

22

اَللّٰهُمَّ صَلِّ وَسَلِّمْ أَشْرَفَ الصَّلٰوةِ وَالتَّسْلِيْمِ عَلٰى حَبِيْبِكَ سَيِّدِنَا وَ نَبِيِّنَا مُحَمَّدٍ عَبْدِكَ وَ رَسُوْلِكَ الَّذِىْ هُوَ أَوَّلُ شَافِعٍ وَ أَوَّلُ مُشَفَّعٍ حَيْثُ قَالَ عَنْ نَفْسِهٖ

﴿ أَنَا أَوَّلُ شَافِعٍ وَ أَوَّلُ مُشَفَّعٍ ﴾

O Allāh! Confer the noblest peace and blessings on your beloved, our master and prophet Muḥammad Your slave and messenger, the one who is the first to intercede and the first whose intercession will be accepted as he himself said "I will be the first to intercede and the first whose intercession will be accepted".

The Ḥabīb (beloved) of Allāh ﷺ will be the intercessor of the Gathering (on the day of judgement) with the permission of Allāh. The intercession will be more than once and of different types.[69]

وَ آخِرُ دَعْوَانَا أَنِ الْحَمْدُ لِلّٰهِ رَبِّ الْعَالَمِيْنَ

---

69 Muslim & Abu Naʻīm

Day Five

1

بِسْمِ اللهِ الرَّحْمٰنِ الرَّحِيْمِ

اَلْحَمْدُ لِلهِ رَبِّ الْعٰلَمِيْنَ ۞ الرَّحْمٰنِ الرَّحِيْمِ ۞ مٰلِكِ يَوْمِ الدِّيْنِ ۞ إِيَّاكَ نَعْبُدُ وَإِيَّاكَ نَسْتَعِيْنُ ۞ اِهْدِنَا الصِّرَاطَ الْمُسْتَقِيْمَ ۞ صِرَاطَ الَّذِيْنَ أَنْعَمْتَ عَلَيْهِمْ غَيْرِ الْمَغْضُوْبِ عَلَيْهِمْ وَلَا الضَّآلِّيْنَ ۞

2

اَللّٰهُمَّ صَلِّ وَسَلِّمْ أَشْرَفَ الصَّلٰوةِ وَالتَّسْلِيْمِ عَلٰى حَبِيْبِكَ سَيِّدِنَا وَنَبِيِّنَا مُحَمَّدٍ عَبْدِكَ وَرَسُوْلِكَ النَّبِيِّ الْأُمِّيِّ نَبِيِّ الرَّحْمَةِ الَّذِيْ قُلْتَ فِيْ حَقِّهِ

﴿ وَمَآ أَرْسَلْنٰكَ إِلَّا رَحْمَةً لِّلْعٰلَمِيْنَ ﴾

سُوْرَةُ الْاَنْبِيَاء

77

O Allāh! Confer the noblest peace and blessings on your beloved, our master and prophet Muḥammad Your slave, messenger, the unlettered prophet and the prophet of mercy as You have declared that "And We have not sent you but as (raḥma) mercy for all the worlds."

This raḥma (mercy) is general and encompasses believers, disbelievers and the entire creation. However, (according to another verse of the Qurān) he is specifically for believers رَءُوْفٌ very kind and رَحِيْمٌ very merciful.

3

$$ اَللّٰهُمَّ أَلْهِمْنِي رُشْدِي وَأَعِذْنِي مِنْ شَرِّ نَفْسِي $$

O Allāh! Inspire in me guidance and deliver me from the evils within myself.

A beautiful duʿā for thinking correctly and it is protection from the evils of the nafs.[70]

4

$$ اَللّٰهُمَّ إِنِّي أَسْأَلُكَ حُبَّكَ وَحُبَّ مَنْ يُحِبُّكَ وَالْعَمَلَ الَّذِي يُبَلِّغُنِي حُبَّكَ $$

O Allāh, I ask You for Your love and love for those who love You and for actions which will bring Your love to me.

---

[70] Tirmidhi & Nasāi

Through this du'ā imān, righteous deeds and the love of Allāh
ﷻ is sought. The cause of ikhlās (sincerety) is love and it makes
performance of deeds easy.[71]

5

اَللّٰهُمَّ اجْعَلْ حُبَّكَ أَحَبَّ إِلَيَّ مِنْ نَفْسِي وَأَهْلِي وَمِنَ الْمَاءِ الْبَارِدِ

O Allāh! Make my love for you dearer to me
than myself, my family, and cold refreshing water.[72]

6

اَللّٰهُمَّ ارْزُقْنِي حُبَّكَ وَحُبَّ مَنْ يَنْفَعُنِي حُبُّهُ عِنْدَكَ

O Allāh! Grant me Your love, and the love of a person whom my
loving him will be of benefit to me near You.[73]

7

اَللّٰهُمَّ فَكَمَا رَزَقْتَنِي مِمَّا أُحِبُّ فَاجْعَلْهُ قُوَّةً لِّي فِيمَا تُحِبُّ اللّٰهُمَّ وَمَا
زَوَيْتَ عَنِّي مِمَّا أُحِبُّ فَاجْعَلْهُ فَرَاغًا لِي فِيمَا تُحِبُّ

O Allāh! The way that you have granted me those things that I love,
employ all those things in whatever you love. O Allāh! Those

---

71 Tirmidhi
72 Tirmidhi & Mustadrak Hākim
73 Tirmidhi

79

bounties that I love and you have withheld them from me, empty my hearts from the thoughts of those bounties and utilise those bounties in whatever you love.

By means of these duʿās one attains peace and tranquillity in the heart. It gets rid of greed and creates contentment.[74]

8

يَا مُقَلِّبَ الْقُلُوبِ ثَبِّتْ قَلْبِي عَلٰى دِيْنِكَ

O turner of the hearts, make my heart steadfast on your dīn.

This is a beautiful duʿā for steadfastness on dīn.[75]

9

اَللّٰهُمَّ إِنِّي أَسْأَلُكَ إِيْمَانًا لَا يَرْتَدُّ وَ نَعِيْمًا لَا يَنْفَدُ وَ مُرَافَقَةَ نَبِيِّنَا (وَ سَيِّدِنَا) مُحَمَّدٍ صَلَّى اللّٰهُ تَعَالٰى عَلَيْهِ وَ اٰلِهِ وَ سَلَّمَ فِي أَعْلٰى دَرَجَةِ جَنَّةِ الْخُلْدِ

O Allāh! I ask you for such imān that does not waver and bounty that does not diminish and the companionship of our Prophet (and

---

74 Tirmidhi
75 Tirmidhi & Nasāi

80

master) (peace and blessings be upon him and his family) in the highest stations of the everlasting Janna.

This is a beautiful masnūn duʿā for protection of imān and continuety of bounties.[76]

10

اَللّٰهُمَّ صَلِّ وَسَلِّمْ اَشْرَفَ الصَّلٰوةِ وَالتَّسْلِيْمِ عَلٰى حَبِيْبِكَ سَيِّدِنَا وَ

نَبِيِّنَا مُحَمَّدٍ عَبْدِكَ وَرَسُوْلِكَ الَّذِیْ جَعَلْتَ طَاعَتَهٗ عَيْنَ طَاعَتِكَ حَيْثُ

قُلْتَ

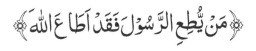

﴿ مَنْ يُّطِعِ الرَّسُوْلَ فَقَدْ اَطَاعَ اللهَ ﴾

سُوْرَةُ النِّسَاء

O Allāh! Confer the noblest peace and blessings on your beloved, our master and prophet Muḥammad Your slave and messenger the one whose obedience you have made Your obedience, as you have declared "Whoever obeys the Messenger obeys Allāh".

The status of Rasulullāh ﷺ is so so exalted in the sight of Allāh ﷻ, that He has made the Prophet's ﷺ obedience as his own obedience.

---

76 Ibn Ḥibbān & Nasāi

11

اَللّٰهُمَّ إِنِّي ضَعِيفٌ فَقَوِّ فِي رِضَاكَ ضَعْفِي وَخُذْ إِلَى الْخَيْرِ بِنَاصِيَتِي وَاجْعَلِ الْإِسْلَامَ مُنْتَهٰى رِضَايَ

O Allāh! I am weak. Give strength, then, to my weakness by Your pleasure and take me, by my forelock, towards good and make Islam the limit of my desire.

Ḥaḍrat Barīra رَضِيَ اللّٰهُ عَنْهَا was taught this du'ā by Rasulullāh ﷺ.[77]

12

اَللّٰهُمَّ اجْعَلْ أَوْسَعَ رِزْقِكَ عَلَيَّ عِنْدَ كِبَرِ سِنِّي وَانْقِطَاعِ عُمُرِي

O Allāh! Make the most expansive of Your sustenance upon me be at the time of my old age and when my life is beginning to leave me.

This du'ā is narrated from Ḥaḍrat 'Aisha رَضِيَ اللّٰهُ عَنْهَا.[78]

13

اَللّٰهُمَّ اجْعَلْ خَيْرَ عُمُرِي آخِرَهُ وَخَيْرَ عَمَلِي خَوَاتِمَهُ وَخَيْرَ أَيَّامِي يَوْمَ أَلْقَاكَ فِيهِ يَا وَلِيَّ الْإِسْلَامِ وَأَهْلِهِ ثَبِّتْنِي بِهِ حَتَّى أَلْقَاكَ

---

77 Kanzul 'Ummāl
78 Mustadrak Ḥākim

O Allāh! Make the best of my life the end of it, the best of my actions the last of them, the best of my days the day in which I meet You. O the protector of Islam and it's people, make me firm on (Islam) until I meet You.

This is a beautiful du'ā for having a *Husn Khātima* (a good death), which is the most important thing.[79]

14

اَللّٰهُمَّ اِنِّیْ اَسْاَلُكَ غِنَاىَ وَ غِنَا مَوْلَاىَ

O Allāh! I ask You for self-sufficiency and the sufficiency of my associates.

A very concise and comprehensive du'ā of the Prophet ﷺ.[80]

15

اَللّٰهُمَّ اجْعَلْنِیْ صَبُوْرًا وَّ اجْعَلْنِیْ شَكُوْرًا وَّ اجْعَلْنِیْ فِیْ عَیْنِیْ صَغِیْرًا وَّ فِیْ اَعْیُنِ النَّاسِ كَبِیْرًا

O Allāh! make me patient, make me grateful, and make me insignificant in my eyes, and eminent in the eyes of people.

---

79 Ḥiṣn Ḥaṣīn
80 Musnad Aḥmad

A perfect and comprehensive way to ask for patience, gratefulness and humility.[81]

16

اَللّٰهُمَّ إِنِّيْ أَسْأَلُكَ مِنْ فَضْلِكَ وَرَحْمَتِكَ فَإِنَّهُ لَا يَمْلِكُهَا إِلَّا أَنْتَ

O Allāh! I ask you from Your grace and mercy, as no one owns them but You.

This is a duʿā for faḍl (grace) and raḥma (mercy).[82]

17

اَللّٰهُمَّ رَبَّ النَّبِيِّ سَيِّدِنَا مُحَمَّدٍ صَلَّى اللّٰهُ تَعَالَى عَلَيْهِ وَاٰلِهٖ وَسَلَّمَ اغْفِرْ لِيْ ذَنْبِيْ وَأَذْهِبْ غَيْظَ قَلْبِيْ وَأَجِرْنِيْ مِنْ مُضِلَّاتِ الْفِتَنِ مَا أَحْيَيْتَنَا

O Allāh! Lord of the Prophet (our master) Muḥammad ﷺ, forgive my sins and remove anger from my heart and protect me from those trials that leads one astray, as long as you keep me alive.

This is a superb duʿā for protection from uncontrollable and excessive anger and tribulations. Rasulullāh ﷺ taught this duʿā to Ḥaḍrat Umm Salama رَضِيَ اللّٰهُ عَنْهَا on her request.[83]

---

81 Musnad Bazzār
82 Tabarāni
83 Musnad Aḥmad

18

اَللّٰهُمَّ إِنِّيْ أَعُوْذُ بِعِزَّتِكَ لَا إِلٰهَ إِلَّا أَنْتَ أَنْ تُضِلَّنِيْ أَنْتَ الْحَيُّ الَّذِيْ لَا

يَمُوْتُ وَالْجِنُّ وَالْإِنْسُ يَمُوْتُوْنَ

O Allāh! I seek refuge in Your honour. There is none worthy of worship but You who is able to lead me astray. You are alive and you never die, while the jinn and humans all die.

This is also a duʿā of the Prophet ﷺ.[84]

19

أَسْتَغْفِرُ اللهَ الَّذِيْ لَا إِلٰهَ إِلَّا هُوَ الْحَيُّ الْقَيُّوْمُ وَأَتُوْبُ إِلَيْهِ

I seek the forgiveness of Allāh, Whom there is none worthy of worship except Him, the Living, the All-Sustaining, and I repent to Him.

This istighfār is a means of forgiving sins even if they may be as much as the foam on the sea.[85] This is because it contains istighfār, tawba, tawhīd and the Ismul A'ẓam.

20

اَللّٰهُمَّ إِنَّا نَسْئَلُكَ مِنْ خَيْرِ مَا سَئَلَكَ مِنْهُ نَبِيُّكَ (سَيِّدُنَا) مُحَمَّدٌ صَلَّى

اللهُ عَلَيْهِ وَالِهِ وَسَلَّمَ وَنَعُوْذُ بِكَ مِنْ شَرِّ مَا اسْتَعَاذَ مِنْهُ نَبِيُّكَ (سَيِّدُنَا)

---

84 Bukhāri & Muslim
85 Abu Dawūd & Tirmidhi

مُحَمَّدٌ صَلَّى اللهُ عَلَيْهِ وَ اللهِ وَسَلَّمَ وَ أَنْتَ الْمُسْتَعَانُ وَعَلَيْكَ الْبَلاَغُ وَلاَ
حَوْلَ وَلاَ قُوَّةَ إِلاَّ بِاللهِ

O Allāh! Indeed we ask You of all good that Your Prophet (our master) Muḥammad ﷺ asked You of, and we seek refuge in You from all evil that Your Prophet (our master) Muḥammad ﷺ sought refuge from. You are the one whose help is sought and the one to make it reach (us); there is no power and strength except with Allāh.

21

اَللّٰهُمَّ صَلِّ وَسَلِّمْ أَشْرَفَ الصَّلوٰةِ وَ التَّسْلِيْمِ عَلٰى حَبِيْبِكَ سَيِّدِنَا وَ
نَبِيِّنَا مُحَمَّدٍ عَبْدِكَ وَ رَسُوْلِكَ الَّذِىْ قَالَ عَنْ نَفْسِهِ ''لاَ يُؤْمِنُ أَحَدُ كُمْ
حَتّٰى أَكُوْنَ أَحَبَّ إِلَيْهِ مِنْ وَلَدِهِ وَ وَالِدِهِ وَ النَّاسِ أَجْمَعِيْنَ''

O Allāh! Confer the noblest peace and blessings on your beloved, our master and prophet Muḥammad Your slave and messenger, the one who said about himself that "None of you will have faith until he loves me more than his father, his children and all mankind."

Imān is dependant on the of love of the blessed person of Rasulullāh ﷺ.[86]

وَ آخِرُ دَعْوَانَا أَنِ الْحَمْدُ لِلّٰهِ رَبِّ الْعَالَمِيْنَ

---

[86] Bukhāri & Muslim

Day Six

1

بِسْمِ اللهِ الرَّحْمٰنِ الرَّحِيْمِ

اَلْحَمْدُ لِلّٰهِ رَبِّ الْعٰلَمِيْنَ ۞ الرَّحْمٰنِ الرَّحِيْمِ ۞ مٰلِكِ يَوْمِ الدِّيْنِ ۞ إِيَّاكَ نَعْبُدُ وَإِيَّاكَ نَسْتَعِيْنُ ۞ اِهْدِنَا الصِّرَاطَ الْمُسْتَقِيْمَ ۞ صِرَاطَ الَّذِيْنَ أَنْعَمْتَ عَلَيْهِمْ غَيْرِ الْمَغْضُوْبِ عَلَيْهِمْ وَلَا الضَّآلِّيْنَ ۞

2

اَللّٰهُمَّ صَلِّ وَسَلِّمْ أَشْرَفَ الصَّلٰوةِ وَالتَّسْلِيْمِ عَلٰى حَبِيْبِكَ سَيِّدِنَا وَ نَبِيِّنَا مُحَمَّدٍ عَبْدِكَ وَرَسُوْلِكَ الرَّؤُوْفِ الرَّحِيْمِ الَّذِيْ قُلْتَ فِيْ حَقِّهِ

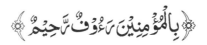

سُوْرَةُ التّوبَة

O Allāh! Confer the noblest peace and blessings on your beloved, our
master and prophet Muḥammad Your slave and the very kind and

very merciful messenger as You have declared that "for the believers he is very kind, very merciful."

The names رَءُوْفٌ *very kind* and رَحِيْمٌ *very merciful* are from the beautiful names of Allāh ﷻ and are in the accordance with the divinity of Allāh ﷻ. But in the verse above it is used for the praising of his beloved Prophet ﷺ in accordance to his exalted status as a slave of Allāh.

3

$$اَللّٰهُمَّ لَا عَيْشَ إِلَّا عَيْشُ الْآخِرَةِ$$

O Allāh, there is no life except the life of the hereafter.

Rasulullāh ﷺ recited this duʿā when he was digging the trench around Madīna during the Battle of Khandaq. [87]

4

$$اَللّٰهُمَّ أَحْيِنِي مِسْكِيْنًا وَّ أَمِتْنِي مِسْكِيْنًا وَّ احْشُرْنِي فِيْ زُمْرَةِ الْمَسَاكِيْنِ$$

O Allāh! Make me live as a miskīn (very poor), die as a miskīn and reserruct me among the company of the masākīn.

This is a duʿā of the Prophet ﷺ for tawāduʿ (humility). [88]

---

87 Bukhāri & Muslim
88 Ibn Māja

5

اَللّٰهُمَّ اجْعَلْنِي مِنَ الَّذِينَ إِذَا أَحْسَنُوا اسْتَبْشَرُوا وَإِذَا أَسَآءُوا اسْتَغْفَرُوا

O Allāh! Make me among those who, when they commit an act of virtue, are overjoyed, and when they commit a mistake, they seek forgiveness.

This is a masnūn du'ā. This should be the constant condition of a believer.[89]

6

اَللّٰهُمَّ وَاقِيَةً كَوَاقِيَةِ الْوَلِيدِ

O Allāh! Protect (me), like you protect a baby.

A masnūn du'ā where one is asking for help with complete and utter feebleleness.[90]

7

اَللّٰهُمَّ إِنَّا نَسْأَلُكَ قُلُوبًا أَوَّاهَةً مُخْبِتَةً مُنِيبَةً فِي سَبِيلِكَ

O Allāh! Indeed we ask You for a heart that expresses sorrow and humiliates itself when it turns towards you in Your path.

---

89 Ibn Māja & Shu'abul Imān
90 Musnad Abi Ya'lā

This duʿā is for the attainment of these qualities, each of which have a great reward.[91]

8

اَللّٰهُمَّ اجْعَلْ حُبَّكَ أَحَبُّ الْأَشْيَاءِ إِلَيَّ وَ اجْعَلْ خَشْيَتَكَ أَخْوَتَ الْأَشْيَاءِ

عِنْدِيْ وَ اقْطَعْ عَنِّيْ حَاجَاتِ الدُّنْيَا بِالشَّوْقِ إِلٰى لِقَائِكَ وَ إِذَا أَقْرَرْتَ

أَعْيُنَ أَهْلِ الدُّنْيَا مِنْ دُنْيَاهُمْ فَأَقِرّ عَيْنِيْ مِنْ عِبَادَتِكَ

O Allāh! Make my love for You the most beloved thing to me, and my fear for You the most fearful thing to me, and remove from me all worldly needs and wants by instilling a passion for meeting You, and when You cooled the eyes of the worldly people (by giving them dunyā), make the coolness of my eyes in worshipping You.[92]

9

اَللّٰهُمَّ لَكَ الْحَمْدُ شُكْرًا وَّ لَكَ الْمَنُّ فَضْلًا

O Allāh! For you is all praise in thankfulness and for you is all benevolence in graciousness.[93]

---

91 Mustadrak Ḥākim
92 Ḥilya Abu Naʿīm
93 Jāmiʿ Ṣaghīr

10

اَللّٰهُمَّ إِنِّي أَسْأَلُكَ التَّوْفِيقَ لِمَحَابِّكَ مِنَ الْأَعْمَالِ وَصِدْقَ

التَّوَكُّلِ عَلَيْكَ وَحُسْنَ الظَّنِّ بِكَ

O Allāh! Indeed I ask You for the ability to do those actions that are beloved to You, (and grant me) true reliance on You and good expectations of You.

This is an excellent masnūn du'ā for asking virtuous qualities.[94]

11

اَللّٰهُمَّ صَلِّ وَسَلِّمْ أَشْرَفَ الصَّلٰوةِ وَالتَّسْلِيمِ عَلٰى حَبِيبِكَ سَيِّدِنَا وَ

نَبِيِّنَا مُحَمَّدٍ عَبْدِكَ وَرَسُولِكَ الَّذِى نَهَيْتَ الْمُؤْمِنِيْنَ اَنْ يَّرْفَعُوْا

اَصْوَاتَهُمْ فَوْقَ صَوْتِهِ حَيْثُ قُلْتَ فِى حَقِّهِ ۞ يَاۤيُّهَا الَّذِيْنَ اٰمَنُوْا لَا

تَرْفَعُوْۤا اَصْوَاتَكُمْ فَوْقَ صَوْتِ النَّبِيِّ ۞

الْحُجَرَات

O Allāh! Confer the noblest peace and blessings on your beloved, our master and prophet Muḥammad Your slave and messenger,

---

94 Ḥilya Abu Na'īm

regarding whom You have prevented the believer from raising their voices above his voice as You have declared "O you who believe, do not raise your voices above the voice of the Prophet."

In this verse believers are ordered to show the highest level of manners and reverence for Rasulullāh ﷺ. The sura also contains a severe warning for even slight disobedience.

12

اَللّٰهُمَّ افْتَحْ مَسَامِعَ قَلْبِيْ لِذِكْرِكَ وَارْزُقْنِيْ طَاعَتَكَ وَطَاعَةَ رَسُوْلِكَ وَعَمَلًا بِكِتَابِكَ

O Allāh! Open the ears of my heart for Your remembrance, and grant me (the ability to be) completely obedient to You, and obedient to Your messenger (peace be upon him), and act in accordance with Your book.

This is a masnūn du'ā for the ability to make dhikr and be obedient.[95]

13

اَللّٰهُمَّ اعْفُ عَنِّيْ فَإِنَّكَ عَفُوٌّ كَرِيْمٌ

O Allāh, pardon me because indeed You are the one who pardons greatly and are the most kind and generous.[96]

---

95 Mu'jamul Awsat
96 Mu'jamul Awsat

14

اَللّٰهُمَّ طَهِّرْ قَلْبِيْ مِنَ النِّفَاقِ وَ عَمَلِيْ مِنَ الرِّيَاءِ وَلِسَانِيْ مِنَ الْكَذِبِ وَ
عَيْنِيْ مِنَ الْخِيَانَةِ فَإِنَّكَ تَعْلَمُ خَائِنَةَ الْأَعْيُنِ وَ مَا تُخْفِي الصُّدُوْرُ

*O Allāh! Purify my heart from hypocrisy, my deeds from any kind of
ostentation, my tongue from lying, and my eye from treachery. For
indeed only You know the treachery of the eyes and what lays hidden
in the breasts.*

A masnūn duʿā for the purification of the heart and
uprightness.[97]

15

اَللّٰهُمَّ إِنِّيْ أَتَّخِذُ عِنْدَكَ عَهْدًا لَّنْ تُخْلِفَنِيْهِ فَإِنَّمَا أَنَا بَشَرٌ فَأَيُّمَا مُؤْمِنٍ
آذَيْتُهُ أَوْ شَتَمْتُهُ أَوْ جَلَدْتُهُ أَوْ لَعَنْتُهُ فَاجْعَلْهَا لَهُ صَلَاةً وَّ زَكَاةً وَّ قُرْبَةً
تُقَرِّبُهُ بِهَا إِلَيْكَ

*O Allāh! I pledge a covenant with You (which I know) that you will
not contravene. I am a human being and thus for any Muslim whom
I have harmed, scolded, cursed or beaten, make this (duʿā) a source of
blessing, purification and nearness to You.*

---

97 Nawādir Uṣūl

An excellent du'ā for absolving one self from those rights of the slaves of Allāh that are due, but one is unable to fulfil them.[98]

16

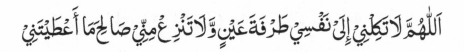

O Allāh! Do not leave me to myself even for the blink of an eye and do not deprive me from any righteousness that You have granted me.

This is a masnūn du'ā for steadfastness.[99]

17

اَللّٰهُمَّ قِنِيْ شَرَّ نَفْسِيْ وَاعْزِمْ لِيْ عَلٰى اَرْشَدِ اَمْرِيْ

O Allāh save me from the evil of myself and give me the determination to act in my affairs in the most rightly guided way.

An excellent du'ā for protection from the evils of the self and for guidance.[100]

18

اَللّٰهُمَّ اغْفِرْ لِيْ وَارْحَمْنِيْ وَتُبْ عَلَيَّ اِنَّكَ اَنْتَ التَّوَّابُ الرَّحِيْمُ

---

98 Bukhārī & Muslim
99 Jāmi' Ṣaghīr
100 Ibn Hibbān

O Allāh! Forgive me, have mercy on me and accept my repentance.
Truly, You are the one who accepts repentance, the Most Merciful. [101]

19

اَللّٰهُمَّ اغْفِرْ لِيْ جِدِّيْ وَهَزْلِيْ وَخَطَئِيْ وَعَمْدِيْ وَكُلَّ ذٰلِكَ عِنْدِيْ

O Allāh! Forgive me my sins done intentionally, those done in jest,
those done mistakenly and all those sins that are with me.

Forgiveness is sought through this du'ā for all types of sins. [102]

20

اَللّٰهُمَّ لَكَ الْحَمْدُ كَالَّذِيْ تَقُوْلُ وَخَيْرًا مِّمَّا نَقُوْلُ

O Allāh, for You is all praise as You have stated better than what we
said. [103]

21

اَللّٰهُمَّ إِنَّا نَسْئَلُكَ مِنْ خَيْرِ مَا سَئَلَكَ مِنْهُ نَبِيُّكَ (سَيِّدُنَا) مُحَمَّدٌ صَلَّى

اللهُ عَلَيْهِ وَاٰلِهِ وَسَلَّمَ وَنَعُوْذُ بِكَ مِنْ شَرِّ مَا اسْتَعَاذَ مِنْهُ نَبِيُّكَ (سَيِّدُنَا)

---

101 The Four Sunan
102 Bukhārī & Muslim
103 Tirmidhi

مُحَمَّدٌ صَلَّى اللهُ عَلَيْهِ وَالِهِ وَسَلَّمَ وَ اَنْتَ الْمُسْتَعَانُ وَعَلَيْكَ الْبَلَاغُ وَلَا حَوْلَ وَلَا قُوَّةَ إِلَّا بِاللهِ [104]

22

اَللّٰهُمَّ صَلِّ وَسَلِّمْ اَشْرَفَ الصَّلٰوةِ وَ التَّسْلِيْمِ عَلٰى حَبِيْبِكَ سَيِّدِنَا وَ نَبِيِّنَا مُحَمَّدٍ عَبْدِكَ وَرَسُوْلِكَ الَّذِىْ اَقْسَمْتَ لَهُ حَيْثُ قُلْتَ جَلَّ شَانُكَ

﴿ وَالضُّحٰى ۞ وَالَّيْلِ إِذَا سَجٰى ۞ مَا وَدَّعَكَ رَبُّكَ وَمَا قَلٰى ۞ وَلَلْاٰخِرَةُ خَيْرٌ لَّكَ مِنَ الْأُوْلٰى ۞ وَلَسَوْفَ يُعْطِيْكَ رَبُّكَ فَتَرْضٰى ﴾

سُوْرَةُ الضُّحٰى

O Allāh! Confer the noblest peace and blessings on Your beloved, our master and prophet Muḥammad Your slave and messenger, regarding whom You have taken oaths as You (whose status is sublime) have said "I swear by the forenoon. And by the night when it becomes peaceful. Your Lord (O Prophet,) has neither forsaken you, nor has become displeased. Surely the Hereafter is much better for

---

104 Tirmidhi

you than the present life. And of course, your Lord will give you so much that you will be pleased."

يُعْطِيْكَ رَبُّكَ داس تساں   فَتَرْضٰی تھیں پوری آس اساں

بچال کریسی پاس اساں   وَاشْفَعْ تُشَفَّعْ صَحِیح پڑھایا

You (O Holy Prophet) have been blessed (by Allāh) with the promise to grant your desire (in full);

And we (your humble followers) have full faith in Allāh's assurance that you will be well-pleased with the bounty of Allāh.

The Gracious One (we hope) shall declare us successful (in the test of earthly life);
Because we have correctly understood the Divine words: "Intercede and thy intercession shall be accepted".

وَ اٰخِرُ دَعْوَانَاۤ اَنِ الْحَمْدُ لِلّٰهِ رَبِّ الْعَالَمِیْنَ

Day Seven

1

بِسْمِ اللهِ الرَّحْمٰنِ الرَّحِيمِ

ٱلْحَمْدُ لِلّٰهِ رَبِّ الْعٰلَمِينَ ۞ الرَّحْمٰنِ الرَّحِيمِ ۞ مٰلِكِ يَوْمِ الدِّينِ ۞ إِيَّاكَ نَعْبُدُ وَإِيَّاكَ نَسْتَعِينُ ۞ اِهْدِنَا الصِّرَاطَ الْمُسْتَقِيمَ ۞ صِرَاطَ الَّذِينَ أَنْعَمْتَ عَلَيْهِمْ غَيْرِ الْمَغْضُوبِ عَلَيْهِمْ وَلَا الضَّآلِّينَ ۞

2

اَللّٰهُمَّ صَلِّ وَسَلِّمْ أَشْرَفَ الصَّلٰوةِ وَالتَّسْلِيمِ عَلٰى حَبِيبِكَ سَيِّدِنَا وَ نَبِيِّنَا مُحَمَّدٍ عَبْدِكَ وَرَسُولِكَ الَّذِى كَانَ وَجْهُهُ

يَتَلَأْلَأُ كَالْقَمَرِ لَيْلَةَ الْبَدْرِ

O Allāh! Confer the noblest peace and blessings on Your beloved, our master and prophet Muḥammad Your slave and messenger, the one whose countenance shines like the full moon. [105]

---

[105] Shifā of Qāḍi Iyāḍ

3

$$اَللّٰهُمَّ اغْفِرْ لِيْ ذَنْبِيْ وَسِّعْ لِيْ خُلُقِيْ وَطَيِّبْ لِيْ كَسْبِيْ وَقَنِّعْنِيْ بِمَا$$

$$رَزَقْتَنِيْ وَلَا تُذْهِبْ طَلَبِيْ إِلٰى شَيْءٍ صَرَفْتَهُ عَنِّيْ اللّٰهُ أَكْبَرُ اللّٰهُ أَكْبَرُ اللّٰهُ$$

$$أَكْبَرُ$$

O Allāh! Forgive my sins and make my character generous, give me contentment in what You have provided me and do not make me seek those things that You have turned away from me. Allāh is the greatest. Allāh is the greatest. Allāh is the greatest.

This is a comprehensive duʿā for the well being and success of this life and the hereafter. Rasulullāh ﷺ offered Ḥaḍrat ʿAli ؓ five thousand goats or five phrases, by means of which he will achieve the success of dīn and dunya. Ḥaḍrat ʿAli ؓ said that five thousand goats were a great deal (in a material sense). But he chose to be taught these five phrases. Then Rasulullāh ﷺ taught him this duʿā.[106]

4

$$اَللّٰهُمَّ حَبِّبِ الْمَوْتَ إِلٰى مَنْ يَعْلَمُ أَنَّ سَيِّدَنَا مُحَمَّدًا صَلَّى اللهُ عَلَيْهِ وَالِهِ$$

$$وَسَلَّمَ رَسُوْلُكَ$$

---

106 Kanzul ʾUmmāl

O Allāh! Make death beloved to whoever that has conviction that our Master Muḥammad (peace and blessings be upon him) is Your messenger.

This duʿā is to remove the fear of death from the believers.[107]

5

اَللّٰهُمَّ اجْعَلْ وَسَاوِسَ قَلْبِيْ خَشْيَتَكَ وَذِكْرَكَ وَاجْعَلْ هِمَّتِيْ

وَهَوَاىَ فِيْمَا تُحِبُّ وَتَرْضٰى

O Allāh! Make the whispers of my heart Your fear and remembrance and make my motivation and desire those things that You love and are pleased with.

This is an excellent duʿā to change evil thoughts to good thoughts.[108]

6

اَللّٰهُمَّ بَارِكْ لِيْ فِي الْمَوْتِ وَفِيْ مَا بَعْدَ الْمَوْتِ

O Allāh! Bless me in my death and in what is after death.

---

107 Jāmi' Ṣaghīr
108 Al Kalimah Al Tayyib

In a long hadīth it is narrated from Ḥaḍrat ʿAisha رضى الله عنها states that whoever read this duʿā 25 times, will receive the status and reward of a martyr.[109]

7

$$ اَللّٰهُمَّ اَذْهِبْ عَنِّى الْهَمَّ وَ الْحُزْنَ $$

O Allāh! Remove from me worry and grief.

To recite this duʿā after Fard ṣalāt and saying Bismillah while placing the right hand on the forhead is sunna.[110]

8

$$ اَللّٰهُمَّ اَعْطِ سَيِّدِنَا مُحَمَّدَانِ الْوَسِيلَةَ وَ اجْعَلْ فِى الْمُصْطَفَيْنَ مَحَبَّتَهُ وَ فِى الْاَعْلَيْنَ دَرَجَتَهُ وَ فِى الْمُقَرَّبِيْنَ ذِكْرَهُ $$

O Allāh, grant our master Muḥammad the wasīla,[111] make him beloved among Your chosen ones, grant him a status among the high ranking ones and make him remembered among the near-ones (to Allāh ﷻ).

If this duʿā is made after every ṣalāt, intercession will become incumbent.[112]

---

109 Majmuʿaz Zawāid
110 Ibn Sunni
111 The highest level in paradise.
112 Kanzul ʿUmmāl

9

اَللّٰهُمَّ اَعْطِنِيْ أَفْضَلَ مَا تُؤْتِيْ عِبَادَكَ الصَّالِحِيْنَ

O Allāh, grant me the best of what You grant to Your righteous slaves.

By reciting this when standing in ṣaff (rows) for ṣalāt, the reciter receives the reward of martyrdom.[113]

10

اَللّٰهُمَّ افْتَحْ أَقْفَالَ قُلُوْبِنَا بِذِكْرِكَ وَ أَتْمِمْ عَلَيْنَا نِعْمَتَكَ مِنْ فَضْلِكَ وَ

اجْعَلْنَا مِنْ عِبَادِكَ الصَّالِحِيْنَ

O Allāh! open the locks of our hearts by (the grace of) Your remembrance, perfect Your bounties upon us, and complete upon us Your grace and make us among Your righteous slaves.

Rasulullāh ﷺ has said that when the muadhin gives the adhān read this duʿā.[114]

---

113 Al-Adhkār
114 Ibn Sunni

11

اَللّٰهُمَّ اجْعَلْ سَرِيْرَتِيْ خَيْرًا مِّنْ عَلَانِيَتِيْ وَ اجْعَلْ عَلَانِيَتِيْ صَالِحَةً

O Allāh! Make my internal self better than my outward-self and make my internal-self righteous.

This is a beautiful du'ā for external and internal purification. [115]

12

اَللّٰهُمَّ صَلِّ وَسَلِّمْ اَشْرَفَ الصَّلٰوةِ وَ التَّسْلِيْمِ عَلٰى حَبِيْبِكَ سَيِّدِنَا وَ

نَبِيِّنَا مُحَمَّدٍ عَبْدِكَ وَ رَسُوْلِكَ الَّذِىْ تَكَفَّلْتَ بِحِفْظِ دِيْنِهٖ حَيْثُ قُلْتَ

جَلَّ شَانُكَ

﴿ اِنَّا نَحْنُ نَزَّلْنَا الذِّكْرَ وَ اِنَّا لَهٗ لَحٰفِظُوْنَ ﴾

O Allāh! Confer the noblest peace and blessings on Your beloved, our master and prophet Muḥammad Your slave and messenger, the one who You made responsible for the preservation of Your dīn as You (whose status is sublime) have said "We, Ourselves, have sent down the Dhikr (the Qurān), and We are its protectors."

---

115 Tirmidhi

Indeed, fortunate are the ones whom Allāh ﷻ gives tawfeeq to do khidma for the preservation of the dīn of Rasulullāh ﷺ. All of them are working for the sake of Allāh at varying degrees.

13

$$ اَللّٰهُمَّ وَفِّقْنِيْ لِمَا تُحِبُّ وَتَرْضٰى مِنَ الْقَوْلِ وَالْعَمَلِ وَالنِّيَّةِ وَالْهُدٰى إِنَّكَ عَلٰى كُلِّ شَيْءٍ قَدِيْرٌ $$

O Allāh! Grant me the abililty to those things that You love and that are pleasing to You from speech, deeds, actions, intentions and guidance. Indeed You have power over all things.

This is wonderful du'ā for righteous actions.[116]

14

$$ اَللّٰهُمَّ اجْعَلْنِيْ مِمَّنْ تَوَكَّلَ عَلَيْكَ فَكَفَيْتَهُ وَاسْتَهْدَاكَ فَهَدَيْتَهُ وَاسْتَنْصَرَكَ فَنَصَرْتَهُ $$

O Allāh make me among those who solely relied upon You and then You sufficed them, make me from those who sought Your guidance and then You guided them and me from those who sought Your help and You helped them.

---

116 Kanzul 'Ummāl

This duʿā is for inclusion among the pious slaves of Allāh.[117]

15

اَللّٰهُمَّ لَا تُخْزِنِيْ فَإِنَّكَ بِيْ عَالِمٌ وَلَا تُعَذِّبْنِيْ فَإِنَّكَ عَلَيَّ قَادِرٌ

O Allāh! Do not disgrace me for indeed You are all-knowing and do not punish me as You have absolute power over me.

16

اَللّٰهُمَّ أَقْبِلْ بِقَلْبِيْ اِلٰى دِيْنِكَ وَاحْفَظْ مِنْ وَّرَآئِنَا بِرَحْمَتِكَ

O Allāh! Turn my heart to Your dīn and protect us from behind with Your mercy.

An excellent duʿā for seeking ability to do righteous actions and protection.[118]

17

اَللّٰهُمَّ احْرُسْنِيْ بِعَيْنِكَ الَّتِيْ لَا تَنَامُ وَاكْنُفْنِيْ بِرُكْنِكَ الَّذِيْ لَا يُرَامُ وَ ارْحَمْنِيْ بِقُدْرَتِكَ عَلَيَّ فَلَا أَهْلِكُ وَأَنْتَ رَجَآئِيْ فَكَمْ مِنْ نِّعْمَةٍ أَنْعَمْتَ بِهَا عَلَيَّ قَلَّ لَكَ بِهَا شُكْرِيْ وَكَمْ مِّنْ بَلِيَّةٍ ابْتَلَيْتَنِيْ بِهَا قَلَّ

لَكَ بِهَا صَبْرِىْ فَيَا مَنْ قَلَّ عِنْدَ نِعْمَتِهِ شُكْرِىْ فَلَمْ يَحْرُمْنِىْ وَيَا مَنْ قَلَّ

عِنْدَ بَلِيَّتِهِ صَبْرِىْ فَلَمْ يَخْذُلْنِىْ وَيَا مَنْ رَآنِىْ عَلَى الْخَطَايَا فَلَمْ يَفْضَحْنِىْ

يَا ذَا الْمَعْرُوفِ الَّذِىْ لَا يَنْقَضِىْ أَبَدًا وَيَا ذَا النَّعْمَآءِ الَّتِىْ لَا تُحْصٰى أَبَدًا

أَسْأَلُكَ أَنْ تُصَلِّىَ عَلٰى (سَيِّدِنَا) مُحَمَّدٍ صَلَّى اللهُ عَلَيْهِ وَاٰلِهِ وَسَلَّمَ وَعَلٰى

اٰلِ (سَيِّدِنَا) مُحَمَّدٍ (صَلَّى اللهُ عَلَيْهِ وَاٰلِهِ وَسَلَّمَ) وَبِكَ أَدْرَأُ فِىْ نُحُوْرِ

الْأَعْدَآءِ وَالْجَبَابِرَةِ

O Allāh! Guard me with Your eye that does not sleep. Shield me by Your shelter that is incredible. Have mercy on me by Your power that You have over me so that I may not be destroyed and You are my absolute hope. How many bounties You have bestowed upon me and I fell short in my graditude. And how many trials You tested me with and I fell short in my patience. O the one in whose bounties I was ungrateful! Do not deprive me. O the one in whose trials I lacked patience! Do not disgrace me. O the One who saw me commit wrong and did not humiliate me. O the processor of all good that will never perish. O the bestower of such bounties and rewards that can not be counted. I beg You to confer the peace and blessings of (our master) Muḥammad (May Allāh confer Peace and Blessings upon him) and on the family of Muḥammad (May Allāh confer Peace and Blessings upon him). With Your help we repel all enemies and tyrants. [119]

18

$$\text{اَللّٰهُمَّ أَعِنِّيْ عَلٰى غَمَرَاتِ الْمَوْتِ وَسَكَرَاتِ الْمَوْتِ}$$

O Allāh! Help me against the severity and agony of death.

Through this du'ā, relief is sought from agony at the time of death.[120]

19

$$\text{اَللّٰهُمَّ اجْعَلْ نَبِيَّنَا لَنَا فَرَطًا وَّ حَوْضَهٗ لَنَا مَوْرِدًا}$$

O Allāh make our Prophet our emissary and make his pond our watering place.

20

$$\text{اَللّٰهُمَّ اغْفِرْ لِيْ وَارْحَمْنِيْ وَ اَلْحِقْنِيْ بِالرَّفِيْقِ الْأَعْلٰى}$$

O Allāh! Forgive me, have mercy on me and unite me with the most exalted companion.

This is the last du'ā of Rasulullāh ﷺ.[121]

---

120 Tirmidhi
121 Bukhāri & Muslim

21

اَللّٰهُمَّ إِنَّا نَسْئَلُكَ مِنْ خَيْرِ مَا سَئَلَكَ مِنْهُ نَبِيُّكَ (سَيِّدُنَا) مُحَمَّدٌ صَلَّى

اللهُ عَلَيْهِ وَاٰلِهٖ وَسَلَّمَ وَنَعُوْذُبِكَ مِنْ شَرِّ مَا اسْتَعَاذَمِنْهُ نَبِيُّكَ (سَيِّدُنَا)

مُحَمَّدٌ صَلَّى اللهُ عَلَيْهِ وَاٰلِهٖ وَسَلَّمَ وَ اَنْتَ الْمُسْتَعَانُ وَعَلَيْكَ الْبَلَاغُ وَلَا

حَوْلَ وَلَا قُوَّةَ إِلَّا بِاللهِ

22

اَللّٰهُمَّ صَلِّ وَسَلِّمْ اَشْرَفَ الصَّلٰوةِ وَ التَّسْلِيْمِ عَلٰى حَبِيْبِكَ سَيِّدِنَا وَ

نَبِيِّنَا مُحَمَّدٍ عَبْدِكَ وَرَسُوْلِكَ الَّذِىْ خَتَمْتَ بِهِ النُّبُوَّةَ وَ الرِّسَالَةَ حَيْثُ

قُلْتَ فِىْ حَقِّهٖ ﴿مَا كَانَ مُحَمَّدٌ اَبَآ اَحَدٍ مِّنْ رِّجَالِكُمْ وَلٰكِنْ رَّسُوْلَ اللهِ

وَخَاتَمَ النَّبِيّٖنَ﴾

سُوْرَةُ الْاَحْزَاب

O Allāh! Confer the noblest peace and blessings on Your beloved,
our master and prophet Muḥammad Your slave and messenger, upon
whom You sealed the nubuwwa (prophethood) and risāla
(messengership). As You have Yourself declared in regards to him

"Muḥammad is not a father of your men, but he is a messenger of Allāh and the last of the prophets"

In a ḥadīth, Rasulullāh ﷺ has said that there will be no prophet after me. For this reason, even Ḥaḍrat 'Īsā's ﷺ who was raised alive above the heavens, after his second coming or descension will also follow the sharī'a of Rasulullāh ﷺ.

وَآخِرُ دَعْوَانَا أَنِ الْحَمْدُ لِلّٰهِ رَبِّ الْعَالَمِيْنَ

Mukhtaṣar Ṣalātul Tasbīḥ

In the book Ḥayātul Muslimīn of Ḥaḍrat Ḥakīmul Umma Mawlāna Ashraf ʿAli Thanwi رحمةالله there is a small section written by his student the late Grand Mufti of Pakistan Mufti Shafiʿ ʿUthmāni رحمةالله called Najātul Muslimīn. This section contains aʿmāl selected from reliable aḥādīth by means of which our past and future sins will be forgiven. These aʿmāl are so easy and light that even a person with minimal motivation and free time can easily perform them. One of these aʿmāl is mukhtaṣar (shortened) ṣalātul tasbīḥ. The well-known procedure of ṣalātul tasbīḥ is narrated in books such as Faḍāil Dhikr of Ḥaḍrat Mawlāna Muḥammad Zakariyya رحمةالله. Ḥaḍrat Sheikh used to do this aʿmāl as part of his Jumuʿa routine. It involves reading the third kalima three hundred times. However, in some other ḥadīth narrations there is another mode of this ṣalāt by means of which all religious and worldly goals can be achieved. This has also been proven through experience. The mashāikh have referred to this by the name of *ṣalātul tasbīḥ ṣughrā* (minor)."

Imām Aḥmad رحمةالله in his Musnad, Imām Tirmidhi رحمةالله under a chapter dedicated to ṣalātul tasbīḥ, Imām Nasāi رحمةالله in his Sunan, Ibn Khuzayma رحمةالله and Ibn Ḥibban رحمةالله in their Saḥīḥs, Ḥākim رحمةالله in his Mustadrak have narrated that Ḥaḍrat Anas ibn Mālik ؓ has narrated from Ḥaḍrat Umm Sulaym رضىاللهعنها that Rasulullāh ﷺ taught her some words to say during ṣalāt that whatever duʿā she would make after that would get accepted. Those words were سُبْحَانَ اللهِ ten times, اَلْحَمْدُ لِلهِ ten times and اَللهُ اَكْبَرُ ten times.

111

Note: Munāwi ﷺ after narrating this ḥadīth, said that the chain of narration is ṣaḥīḥ. Then he further stated that the benefits and effects of this ṣalāt will become apparent when the words are uttered with understanding of its meaning and with presence of heart not simple movement of the tongue. Allāh ﷻ knows best.

In this ṣalātul tasbīh, there is no special part of ṣalāt that has been specified as to when to read the above phrases. It has not been specified in ḥadīth nor according to any ʿālim or sheikh. Therefore, it is at the discretion of the worshipper as to when they would like to repeat those phrases.

Daily Masnūn Duʿās

Most often recited daily masnūn duʿās

The noble mashāikh and ʿulamā have said that blessed indeed is the person that has made as part of their daily routine duʿās which are specific to a situation. Whatever works they will engage in, they will have baraka in it and Allāh ﷻ will make it easy for them. This person will also be included among those people who make dhikr of Allāh ﷻ excessively. A person will attain the blessing by practicing these duʿās only when the ghafla (negligence) of the heart is removed and the heart has love for and a connection with Allāh ﷻ. To develop this, it is necessary to have:

1.suḥba (companionship/association) of the mashāikh for some time and

2. to practice the adhkār they have prescribed with discipline.

However, without these two things a person with a negligent heart will not recite them when the situation for practicing that duʿā occurs despite him having learnt the virtues of the duʿās, knows of their blessings and memorised its words. For example, saying Bismillah before eating is known to everyone but majority of people forget to say it and the food becomes devoid of baraka. In the following pages the most common occurring duʿās have been compiled. These should be memorised and practically applied.

Duʿā at the adhān of Maghrib

اَللّٰهُمَّ هٰذَا اِقْبَالُ لَيْلِكَ وَ اِدْبَارُ نَهَارِكَ وَاَصْوَاتُ دُعَاتِكَ فَاغْفِرْ لِيْ

Duʿā when entering home

اَللّٰهُمَّ اِنِّيْ اَسْأَلُكَ خَيْرَ الْمَوْلَجِ وَخَيْرَ الْمَخْرَجِ بِسْمِ اللّٰهِ وَلَجْنَا وَبِسْمِ اللّٰهِ

خَرَجْنَا وَعَلَى اللّٰهِ رَبِّنَا تَوَكَّلْنَا

Duʿā before sleeping

اَللّٰهُمَّ بِاسْمِكَ اَمُوْتُ وَاَحْيَا

Duʿā when waking up from sleep

اَلْحَمْدُ لِلّٰهِ الَّذِيْ اَحْيَانَا بَعْدَ مَآ اَمَاتَنَا وَاِلَيْهِ النُّشُوْرُ

Duʿā on entering a toilet

بِسْمِ اللّٰهِ اَللّٰهُمَّ اِنِّيْ اَعُوْذُ بِكَ مِنَ الْخُبُثِ وَالْخَبَآئِثِ

Duʿā for after coming out of the toilet

غُفْرَانَكَ اَلْحَمْدُ لِلّٰهِ الَّذِيْ اَذْهَبَ عَنِّي الْاَذٰى وَعَافَانِيْ

Duʿā before starting wuḍu

بِسْمِ اللّٰهِ الرَّحْمٰنِ الرَّحِيْمِ

115

Duʿā during wuḍu

اَللّٰهُمَّ اغْفِرْ لِي ذَنْبِي وَوَسِّعْ لِي فِي دَارِي وَبَارِكْ لِي فِي رِزْقِي

Duʿā after wuḍu

أَشْهَدُ أَنْ لَّا إِلٰهَ إِلَّا اللهُ وَحْدَهُ لَا شَرِيْكَ لَهُ وَأَشْهَدُ أَنَّ مُحَمَّدًا عَبْدَهُ

وَرَسُولُهُ اللّٰهُمَّ اجْعَلْنِي مِنَ التَّوَّابِيْنَ وَاجْعَلْنِي مِنَ الْمُتَطَهِّرِيْنَ

سُبْحَانَكَ اللّٰهُمَّ وَبِحَمْدِكَ أَشْهَدُ أَنْ لَّا إِلٰهَ إِلَّا أَنْتَ أَسْتَغْفِرُكَ وَأَتُوْبُ

إِلَيْكَ

Duʿā when leaving home

بِسْمِ اللهِ تَوَكَّلْتُ عَلَى اللهِ وَلَا حَوْلَ وَلَا قُوَّةَ إِلَّا بِاللهِ

Duʿā when entering a masjid

بِسْمِ اللهِ وَالصَّلَاةُ وَالسَّلَامُ عَلٰى رَسُوْلِ اللهِ اَللّٰهُمَّ اغْفِرْ لِي ذُنُوْبِي وَ

افْتَحْ لِي أَبْوَابَ رَحْمَتِكَ

Duʿā after leaving a masjid [122]

بِسْمِ اللهِ وَالصَّلَاةُ وَالسَّلَامُ عَلٰى رَسُوْلِ اللهِ اَللّٰهُمَّ اغْفِرْلِيْ ذُنُوْبِيْ وَ افْتَحْ لِيْ أَبْوَابَ فَضْلِكَ

Duʿā after adhān

اَللّٰهُمَّ رَبَّ هٰذِهِ الدَّعْوَةِ التَّآمَّةِ وَالصَّلٰوةِ الْقَآئِمَةِ اٰتِ مُحَمَّدَ الْوَسِيْلَةَ وَالْفَضِيْلَةَ وَابْعَثْهُ مَقَامًا مَّحْمُوْدَا الَّذِىْ وَعَدْتَّهُ اِنَّكَ لَا تُخْلِفُ الْمِيْعَادَ

Duʿā after ṣalāt and after wiping right hand on forehead

بِسْمِ اللهِ الَّذِىْ لَآ اِلٰهَ اِلَّا هُوَ الرَّحْمٰنِ الرَّحِيْمِ اَللّٰهُمَّ اَذْهِبْ عَنِّي الْهَمَّ وَالْحُزْنَ

Duʿā before eating

بِسْمِ اللهِ وَعَلٰى بَرَكَةِ اللهِ

Duʿā after eating

اَلْحَمْدُ لِلّٰهِ الَّذِىْ اَطْعَمَنَا وَسَقَانَا وَجَعَلَنَا الْمُسْلِمِيْنَ

---

122 This increases in rizq i.e. after leaving the masjid if one reads along the way اَللّٰهُمَّ اِنِّيْ اَسْأَلُكَ رِزْقًا وَّاسِعًا and then read ṣalāt on the Prophet ﷺ. اَللّٰهُمَّ اكْفِنَا بِحَلَالِكَ عَنْ حَرَامِكَ وَاَغْنِنَا بِفَضْلِكَ عَمَّنْ سِوَاكَ and حَلَالًا طَيِّبًا

Duʿā by the guest for the host

اَللّٰهُمَّ أَطْعِمْ مَنْ أَطْعَمَنِيْ وَاسْقِ مَنْ سَقَانِيْ

Duʿā when wearing clothes

اَلْحَمْدُ لِلّٰهِ الَّذِيْ كَسَانِيْ مَا أُوَارِيْ بِهِ عَوْرَتِيْ وَأَتَجَمَّلُ بِهِ فِيْ حَيَاتِيْ

Duʿā for farewelling someone on a journey

أَسْتَوْدِعُ اللّٰهَ دِيْنَكَ وَأَمَانَتَكَ وَخَوَاتِيْمَ عَمَلِكَ

Duʿā when someone is about sit /climb on to a transport

بِسْمِ اللّٰهِ

Duʿā after one is seated on their ride

اَلْحَمْدُ لِلّٰهِ سُبْحٰنَ الَّذِيْ سَخَّرَ لَنَا هٰذَا وَمَا كُنَّا لَهُ مُقْرِنِيْنَ ۞ وَإِنَّا إِلٰى

رَبِّنَا لَمُنْقَلِبُوْنَ ۞

Duʿā of returning from a journey

آئِبُوْنَ تَائِبُوْنَ عَابِدُوْنَ لِرَبِّنَا حَامِدُوْنَ

Duʿā when entering a town or city

اللّٰهُمَّ بَارِكْ لَنَا فِيْهَا (3 times) then recite:

118

اَللّٰهُمَّ ارْزُقْنَا جَنَاهَا وَحَبِّبْنَا إِلٰى أَهْلِهَا وَحَبِّبْ صَالِحِيْ أَهْلِهَا إِلَيْنَا

Duʿā when making a stopover on journey

أَعُوْذُ بِكَلِمَاتِ اللّٰهِ التَّامَّاتِ مِنْ شَرِّ مَا خَلَقَ

Duʿā for any calamity

إِنَّا لِلّٰهِ وَإِنَّا إِلَيْهِ رَاجِعُوْنَ اللّٰهُمَّ عِنْدَكَ أَحْتَسِبُ مُصِيْبَتِيْ فَأَجِرْنِيْ فِيْهَا

وَ أَبْدِلْنِيْ مِنْهَا خَيْرًا

Duʿā to make any difficulty easy

اَللّٰهُمَّ لَا سَهْلَ إِلَّا مَا جَعَلْتَهُ سَهْلًا وَّ أَنْتَ تَجْعَلُ الْحَزْنَ سَهْلًا إِذَا شِئْتَ

Duʿā on sigting the crescent of the new month

اَللّٰهُمَّ أَهِلَّهُ عَلَيْنَا بِالْيُمْنِ وَالْإِيْمَانِ وَالسَّلَامَةِ وَالْإِسْلَامِ وَ التَّوْفِيْقِ لِمَا

تُحِبُّ وَتَرْضٰى رَبِّيْ وَرَبُّكَ اللّٰهُ

Duʿā when looking in a mirror

اَللّٰهُمَّ حَسَّنْتَ خَلْقِيْ فَحَسِّنْ خُلُقِيْ

Duʿā when one sees the things one loves

اَلْحَمْدُ لِلّٰهِ الَّذِيْ بِنِعْمَتِهِ تَتِمُّ الصَّالِحَاتُ

Duʿā when one experiences an undesirable situation

اَلْحَمْدُ لِلّٰهِ عَلٰى كُلِّ حَالٍ

Duʿā at the time of anger

اَعُوْذُ بِاللهِ مِنَ الشَّيْطَانِ الرَّجِيْمِ

Duʿā before rising from a gathering

سُبْحَانَ اللهِ وَبِحَمْدِهِ سُبْحَانَكَ اللّٰهُمَّ وَبِحَمْدِكَ أَشْهَدُ أَنْ لَّا إِلٰهَ إِلَّا أَنْتَ أَسْتَغْفِرُكَ وَأَتُوْبُ إِلَيْكَ

Note: These easy duʿās are given as a sample of duʿās that we can learn. In the aḥādīth there is no facet of life except that we have been given guidance for it. If after practicing these duʿās assiduously, one develops an increased fondness and eagerness for duʿā, then Ḥizbul Aʿẓam and Ḥiṣn Ḥaṣīn can also be included in the daily routine.

120

Istikhāra Masnūna

Istikhāra Masnūna

Rasulullah ﷺ has stated that from the good fortune of a person is that he makes istikhāra (seeking of good) in all matters excessively and to be pleased on the decree of Allāh ﷻ. And the misfortune of a person is in not doing istikhāra.

It has been narrated that whoever makes mashwara (consultation according to sunna) for any matter will never have any regret and whoever makes istikhāra will never experience failure.

1. Rasulullāh ﷺ taught the Istikhāra in the following manner i.e. that when a person is in any dilemma or indecision, he should perform two rakāts of nafl ṣalāt and thereafter recite the following duʿā:

اَللّٰهُمَّ إِنِّيْ أَسْتَخِيرُكَ بِعِلْمِكَ وَأَسْتَقْدِرُكَ بِقُدْرَتِكَ وَأَسْأَلُكَ مِنْ فَضْلِكَ الْعَظِيمِ فَإِنَّكَ تَقْدِرُ وَلَا أَقْدِرُ وَتَعْلَمُ وَلَا أَعْلَمُ وَأَنْتَ عَلَّامُ الْغُيُوبِ اَللّٰهُمَّ إِنْ كُنْتَ تَعْلَمُ أَنَّ هَذَا الْأَمْرَ خَيْرٌ لِي فِي دِينِي وَمَعَاشِي وَعَاقِبَةِ أَمْرِي فَاقْدِرْهُ لِي وَيَسِّرْهُ لِي ثُمَّ بَارِكْ لِي فِيهِ وَإِنْ كُنْتَ تَعْلَمُ أَنَّ هَذَا الْأَمْرَ شَرٌّ فِي دِينِي وَمَعَاشِي وَعَاقِبَةِ أَمْرِي فَاصْرِفْهُ عَنِّي وَاصْرِفْنِي عَنْهُ وَاقْدِرْ لِي الْخَيْرَ حَيْثُ كَانَ ثُمَّ أَرْضِنِي بِهِ

*"O Allāh, with Your knowledge I seek the good, with Your power I seek ability and Your mighty favour for certainly You have the power I have none, You know and I do not Know and You Know the unseen. O Allāh, in Your knowledge if **this matter** is good for me in Dunya and the Ākhira, then let it be for me, grant me blessings in it and if **this matter** is bad for me then keep it far away from me and grant good wherever it may be and make me pleased with that".*

2. If one has to make a quick decision for some matter and there is not enough time to pray ṣalāt, then one should turn their heart towards Allāh ﷻ with full attention and read ٱللّٰهُمَّ خِرْلِیْ وَ اخْتَرْلِیْ several times. InshāAllāh the reciter will be guided towards goodness.

Morning and evening awrād [123]

3 times	بِسْمِ اللهِ الَّذِي لَايَضُرُّ مَعَ اسْمِهِ شَيْءٌ فِي الْأَرْضِ وَلَا فِي السَّمَاءِ وَهُوَ السَّمِيعُ الْعَلِيمُ
3 times	أَعُوذُ بِكَلِمَاتِ اللهِ التَّامَّاتِ مِنْ شَرِّ مَا خَلَقَ
3 times	رَضِيتُ بِاللهِ رَبًّا وَبِالْإِسْلَامِ دِينًا وَبِمُحَمَّدٍ ﷺ نَبِيًّا وَرَسُولًا
3 times	حَسْبِيَ اللهُ لَا إِلٰهَ إِلَّا هُوَ عَلَيْهِ تَوَكَّلْتُ وَهُوَ رَبُّ الْعَرْشِ الْعَظِيمِ
7 times	أُفَوِّضُ أَمْرِي إِلَى اللهِ إِنَّ اللهَ بَصِيرٌ بِالْعِبَادِ
Once	اَللّٰهُمَّ أَنْتَ رَبِّي لَا إِلٰهَ إِلَّا أَنْتَ خَلَقْتَنِي وَأَنَا عَبْدُكَ وَأَنَا عَلَى عَهْدِكَ وَوَعْدِكَ مَا اسْتَطَعْتُ أَعُوذُ بِكَ مِنْ شَرِّ مَا صَنَعْتُ أَبُوءُ لَكَ بِنِعْمَتِكَ عَلَيَّ وَأَبُوءُ بِذَنْبِي فَاغْفِرْ لِي فَإِنَّهُ لَا يَغْفِرُ الذُّنُوبَ إِلَّا أَنْتَ
Once	رَبَّنَا آتِنَا مِنْ لَدُنْكَ رَحْمَةً وَهَيِّئْ لَنَا مِنْ أَمْرِنَا رَشَدًا
Once	اَللّٰهُمَّ وَاقِيَةً كَوَاقِيَةِ الْوَلِيدِ اَللّٰهُمَّ اسْتُرْنَا بِسَتْرِكَ الْجَمِيلِ

Istighfār, Kalima Ṭayyiba, third kalima, ṣalawāt should be done a hundred times each. Also, one should be particular about the forty ḥadīth of ṣalawāt and reading Ḥizbul Aʿẓam.

---

123 plural of wird - duʿās for regular reading

124

Reading of the Holy Qurān, Sura Yasīn in the morning and Sura Mulk before sleeping at night, Salāt on the Prophet ﷺ, Sura Fātiha, Ayātul Kursi and the 4 Quls (Kāfirūn, Ikhlās, Falaq and Nās) and then to blow on hands and wipe all over body. Then read Tasbīḥ Fatima and then the duʿās for sleeping. Read Sura Kahf, Ṣalātul Tasbīḥ and make abundant ṣalāt on the Prophet ﷺ on Jumuʿa as has been explained on Page 35 in detail. Ṣalāt on the Prophet should be made abundantly and continuously by a Muslim in every situation. If one is unable to do so due to being engaged in other work or can not be fully attentive then the following concise ṣalāt can be recited:

$$\text{صَلَّى اللهُ عَلَى مُحَمَّدٍ صَلَّى اللهُ عَلَيْهِ وَسَلَّمَ}$$

However, this ṣalāt is only for those people who can not do any ṣalawāt due to extreme inability. As for people under normal circumstances, they should do all their awrād that have been prescribed by their mashāikh. For example, Ḥaḍrat Sheikh's رَحِمَهُ اللّٰه daily adhkār and aʿmāl are handed out on paper to people who are newly initiated into his tarīqa. Similarly, anybody associated with any sheikh should practice the guidelines and advices of their sheikhs. Those who are initiated into a tarīqa are taught various formulas of dhikr and practices over time.

Forty Ḥadīth of Ṣalāt and Salām

Forty Ḥadīth of Ṣalāt and Salām

The noble ʿulamā have said that whenever a slave of Allāh gives preference to what Allāh loves (i.e. sending the blessed ṣalawāt on the Prophet ﷺ over one's own desires and wants, even through duʿā) or that he gives preference to Allāh's pleasure over his own goals, then Allāh fulfils all the needs of this slave.

مَنْ كَانَ لِلّٰهِ كَانَ اللّٰهُ لَهُ

At the end of a narration of Ḥaḍrat ʾUbay bin Kaʿab ؓ in which he asked the noble Prophet ﷺ of what would be the reward if he spent all the time alotted for dhikr for ṣalāt upon the Prophet ﷺ? The Prophet ﷺ said إِذًا تُكْفَى هَمَّكَ وَ يُكَفَّرُ لَكَ ذَنْبَكَ *It will suffice you for all your worries and and it will be expiation for your sins.* In another narration Rasulullāh ﷺ has said that person who sends ṣalāt on me once, Allāh sends on him ṣalāt (blessings and mercy) ten times.

Allāh rewards according to the deed. That is why when someone sends ṣalāt on the Prophet ﷺ profusely, then Allāh sends innumerable mercies and salutations on the person reciting, his kith and kin and his descendants. Those who receive such blessings will have his goals of this world as well as the hereafter fulfilled. The reason is that ṣalawāt are accepted and whoever will make duʿā for their needs during the reading of the following masnūn ṣalawāt will Inshā-Allāh have their duʿās accepted.

The most virtuous ṣalāt

The most rewarding and virtuous ṣalawāt are the ones narrated from Ṣaḥaba ☙, after they requested the beloved of Allāh Rasulullāh ﷺ to teach them and then the Holy Prophet ﷺ uttered those pure words. Out of these, the most virtuous is the that which is commonly known as Durūd or Ṣalāt Ibrāhīmiyya. This ṣalāt is narrated in seven authentic aḥādīth with slight variation in the wording. Some of these were gatherd by Mawlāna Ashraf ʿAli Thānwi ﷾ in the form of forty ḥadīth in the following compilation.

Each ṣalāt and salām is a ḥadīth as well, therefore the one who recites it, reads it to others or dessiminates it, will gain the reward for reciting forty ḥadīth. The reward for doing so is that the person will be reserructed among the ʿulamā on the Day of Judgement and Rasululllah ﷺ will intercede for him i.e. he will have the reward of conveying ḥadīth and the reward of reciting ṣalawāt.

The righteous predecessors have stated that اَللّٰهُمَّ is to call Allāh ﷻ by all His beautiful names at once and حَمِيدٌ مَّجِيدٌ are two such blessed names of Allāh ﷻ that all His attributes are contained therein whether they be His attributes of *beauty* or attributes of *majesty*. Therefore, while reading Ṣalāt Ibrāhīmiyya, the meaning of these names of Allāh ﷻ should be reflected upon. By means of this, the spiritual benefits of the ṣalāt will be increased.

عَلٰى حَبِيبِكَ خَيْرِ الْخَلْقِ كُلِّهِمْ   يَا رَبِّ صَلِّ وَسَلِّمْ دَائِمًا أَبَدًا

بِسْمِ اللهِ الرَّحْمٰنِ الرَّحِيْمِ

سَلٰمٌ عَلٰى عِبَادِهِ الَّذِيْنَ اصْطَفٰى

سَلٰمٌ عَلَى الْمُرْسَلِيْنَ

(القرآن الكريم)

1

اَللّٰهُمَّ صَلِّ عَلٰى مُحَمَّدٍ وَّعَلٰى آلِ مُحَمَّدٍ وَّأَنْزِلْهُ الْمَقْعَدَ الْمُقَرَّبَ عِنْدَكَ يَوْمَ الْقِيَامَةِ [124]

2

اَللّٰهُمَّ رَبَّ هٰذِهِ الدَّعْوَةِ الْقَائِمَةِ وَالصَّلٰوةِ النَّافِعَةِ صَلِّ عَلٰى مُحَمَّدٍ وَّارْضَ عَنِّي رِضًا لَّا تَسْخَطْ بَعْدَهٗ أَبَدًا [125]

3

اَللّٰهُمَّ صَلِّ عَلٰى مُحَمَّدٍ عَبْدِكَ وَرَسُوْلِكَ وَصَلِّ عَلَى الْمُؤْمِنِيْنَ وَالْمُؤْمِنَاتِ وَالْمُسْلِمِيْنَ وَالْمُسْلِمَاتِ [126]

---

124 Rasulullah ﷺ said that "whoever reads this ṣalāt, my intercession becomes incumbent for him." Ṭabarāni

125 Musnad Aḥmad

126 It has been narrated by Abu saʿīd al-Khudri ؓ that Rasulullah ﷺ said that "the person who doesn't have wealth to spend for charity then he should read this ṣalāt and it will be a means of purification for him." Ibn Hibbān

4

اَللّٰهُمَّ صَلِّ عَلٰى مُحَمَّدٍ وَّ عَلٰى آلِ مُحَمَّدٍ وَّبَارِك عَلٰى مُحَمَّدٍ وَّ عَلٰى آلِ

مُحَمَّدٍ وَّارْحَمْ مُحَمَّدًا وَّ آلَ مُحَمَّدٍ كَمَا صَلَّيْتَ وَبَارَكْتَ وَرَحِمْتَ عَلٰى

إِبْرَاهِيمَ وَ عَلٰى آلِ إِبْرَاهِيمَ إِنَّكَ حَمِيدٌ مَّجِيدٌ [127]

5

اَللّٰهُمَّ صَلِّ عَلٰى مُحَمَّدٍ وَّ عَلٰى آلِ مُحَمَّدٍ كَمَا صَلَّيْتَ عَلٰى آلِ إِبْرَاهِيمَ

إِنَّكَ حَمِيدٌ مَّجِيدٌ اَللّٰهُمَّ بَارِك عَلٰى مُحَمَّدٍ وَّ عَلٰى آلِ مُحَمَّدٍ كَمَا بَارَكْتَ

عَلٰى آلِ إِبْرَاهِيمَ إِنَّكَ حَمِيدٌ مَّجِيدٌ [128]

6

اَللّٰهُمَّ صَلِّ عَلٰى مُحَمَّدٍ وَّ عَلٰى آلِ مُحَمَّدٍ كَمَا صَلَّيْتَ عَلٰى آلِ إِبْرَاهِيمَ

إِنَّكَ حَمِيدٌ مَّجِيدٌ وَبَارِك عَلٰى مُحَمَّدٍ وَّ عَلٰى آلِ مُحَمَّدٍ كَمَا بَارَكْتَ عَلٰى

آلِ إِبْرَاهِيمَ إِنَّكَ حَمِيدٌ مَّجِيدٌ [129]

---

127 Bayhaqi
128 Bukhārī Sharīf
129 Muslim Sharīf

7

اَللّٰهُمَّ صَلِّ عَلٰى مُحَمَّدٍ وَّ عَلٰى آلِ مُحَمَّدٍ كَمَا صَلَّيْتَ عَلٰى إِبْرَاهِيْمَ إِنَّكَ

حَمِيْدٌ مَّجِيْدٌ اَللّٰهُمَّ بَارِكْ عَلٰى مُحَمَّدٍ وَّ عَلٰى آلِ مُحَمَّدٍ كَمَا بَارَكْتَ عَلٰى

إِبْرَاهِيْمَ إِنَّكَ حَمِيْدٌ مَّجِيْدٌ

8

اَللّٰهُمَّ صَلِّ عَلٰى مُحَمَّدٍ وَّ عَلٰى آلِ مُحَمَّدٍ كَمَا صَلَّيْتَ عَلٰى إِبْرَاهِيْمَ وَ عَلٰى

آلِ إِبْرَاهِيْمَ إِنَّكَ حَمِيْدٌ مَّجِيْدٌ وَ بَارِكْ عَلٰى مُحَمَّدٍ وَّ عَلٰى آلِ مُحَمَّدٍ كَمَا

بَارَكْتَ عَلٰى إِبْرَاهِيْمَ إِنَّكَ حَمِيْدٌ مَّجِيْدٌ[131]

9

اَللّٰهُمَّ صَلِّ عَلٰى مُحَمَّدٍ وَّ عَلٰى آلِ مُحَمَّدٍ كَمَا صَلَّيْتَ عَلٰى إِبْرَاهِيْمَ وَ

بَارِكْ عَلٰى مُحَمَّدٍ وَّ عَلٰى آلِ مُحَمَّدٍ كَمَا بَارَكْتَ عَلٰى إِبْرَاهِيْمَ إِنَّكَ

حَمِيْدٌ مَّجِيْدٌ[132]

---

130 Ibn Māja
131 Nasāi
132 Abu Dawūd

10

اَللّٰهُمَّ صَلِّ عَلٰى مُحَمَّدٍ وَّ عَلٰى آلِ مُحَمَّدٍ كَمَا صَلَّيْتَ عَلٰى إِبْرَاهِيمَ إِنَّكَ

حَمِيْدٌ مَّجِيْدٌ اَللّٰهُمَّ بَارِكْ عَلٰى مُحَمَّدٍ وَّ عَلٰى آلِ مُحَمَّدٍ كَمَا بَارَكْتَ عَلٰى

آلِ إِبْرَاهِيمَ إِنَّكَ حَمِيْدٌ مَّجِيْدٌ [133]

11

اَللّٰهُمَّ صَلِّ عَلٰى مُحَمَّدٍ وَّ عَلٰى آلِ مُحَمَّدٍ كَمَا صَلَّيْتَ عَلٰى آلِ إِبْرَاهِيمَ وَ

بَارِكْ عَلٰى مُحَمَّدٍ وَّ عَلٰى آلِ مُحَمَّدٍ كَمَا بَارَكْتَ عَلٰى آلِ إِبْرَاهِيمَ فِي

الْعَالَمِيْنَ إِنَّكَ حَمِيْدٌ مَّجِيْدٌ [١٣٤]

12

اَللّٰهُمَّ صَلِّ عَلٰى مُحَمَّدٍ وَّ أَزْوَاجِهٖ وَ ذُرِّيَّتِهٖ كَمَا صَلَّيْتَ عَلٰى آلِ

إِبْرَاهِيمَ وَ بَارِكْ عَلٰى مُحَمَّدٍ وَّ أَزْوَاجِهٖ وَ ذُرِّيَّتِهٖ كَمَا بَارَكْتَ عَلٰى آلِ

إِبْرَاهِيمَ إِنَّكَ حَمِيْدٌ مَّجِيْدٌ [135]

---

133 Abu Dawūd
134 Muslim Sharīf
135 Abu Dawūd

13

اَللّٰهُمَّ صَلِّ عَلٰى مُحَمَّدٍ وَّ عَلٰى أَزْوَاجِهِ وَذُرِّيَّتِهِ كَمَا صَلَّيْتَ عَلٰى آلِ

إِبْرَاهِيْمَ وَبَارِكْ عَلٰى مُحَمَّدٍ وَّ عَلٰى أَزْوَاجِهِ وَذُرِّيَّتِهِ كَمَا بَارَكْتَ عَلٰى

آلِ إِبْرَاهِيْمَ إِنَّكَ حَمِيْدٌ مَّجِيْدٌ [136]

14

اَللّٰهُمَّ صَلِّ عَلٰى مُحَمَّدٍ النَّبِيِّ وَأَزْوَاجِهِ أُمَّهَاتِ الْمُؤْمِنِيْنَ وَذُرِّيَّتِهِ وَ

أَهْلِ بَيْتِهِ كَمَا صَلَّيْتَ عَلٰى إِبْرَاهِيْمَ إِنَّكَ حَمِيْدٌ مَّجِيْدٌ [137]

15

اَللّٰهُمَّ صَلِّ عَلٰى مُحَمَّدٍ وَّ عَلٰى آلِ مُحَمَّدٍ كَمَا صَلَّيْتَ عَلٰى إِبْرَاهِيْمَ وَعَلٰى

آلِ إِبْرَاهِيْمَ وَبَارِكْ عَلٰى مُحَمَّدٍ وَّ عَلٰى آلِ مُحَمَّدٍ كَمَا بَارَكْتَ عَلٰى

إِبْرَاهِيْمَ وَتَرَحَّمْ عَلٰى مُحَمَّدٍ وَّ عَلٰى آلِ مُحَمَّدٍ كَمَا تَرَحَّمْتَ عَلٰى

إِبْرَاهِيْمَ وَعَلٰى آلِ إِبْرَاهِيْمَ [138]

---

136 Muslim Sharīf
137 Ḥaḍrat Abu Hurayra ﷠ narrated that the Prophet ﷺ said "if it pleases a person that he may be rewarded fully for the ṣalāt sent on my household then he should read this ṣalāt." Abu Dawūd
138 Abu Hurayra ﷠ has narrated that Rasulullah ﷺ has said that "whoever reads this ṣalāt, I will bear witness for him on the Day of Judgment and will do his intercession." Tabari

16

اَللّٰهُمَّ صَلِّ عَلٰى مُحَمَّدٍ وَّ عَلٰى آلِ مُحَمَّدٍ كَمَا صَلَّيْتَ عَلٰى إِبْرَاهِيْمَ وَعَلٰى

آلِ إِبْرَاهِيْمَ إِنَّكَ حَمِيْدٌ مَّجِيْدٌ اَللّٰهُمَّ بَارِكْ عَلٰى مُحَمَّدٍ وَّ عَلٰى آلِ مُحَمَّدٍ

كَمَا بَارَكْتَ عَلٰى إِبْرَاهِيْمَ وَعَلٰى آلِ إِبْرَاهِيْمَ إِنَّكَ حَمِيْدٌ مَّجِيْدٌ اَللّٰهُمَّ

تَرَحَّمْ عَلٰى مُحَمَّدٍ وَّ عَلٰى آلِ مُحَمَّدٍ كَمَا تَرَحَّمْتَ عَلٰى إِبْرَاهِيْمَ وَعَلٰى آلِ

إِبْرَاهِيْمَ إِنَّكَ حَمِيْدٌ مَّجِيْدٌ اَللّٰهُمَّ تَحَنَّنْ عَلٰى مُحَمَّدٍ وَّ عَلٰى آلِ مُحَمَّدٍ كَمَا

تَحَنَّنْتَ عَلٰى إِبْرَاهِيْمَ وَعَلٰى آلِ إِبْرَاهِيْمَ إِنَّكَ حَمِيْدٌ مَّجِيْدٌ اَللّٰهُمَّ سَلِّمْ

عَلٰى مُحَمَّدٍ وَّ عَلٰى آلِ مُحَمَّدٍ كَمَا سَلَّمْتَ عَلٰى إِبْرَاهِيْمَ وَعَلٰى آلِ

إِبْرَاهِيْمَ إِنَّكَ حَمِيْدٌ مَّجِيْدٌ[139]

17

اَللّٰهُمَّ صَلِّ عَلٰى مُحَمَّدٍ وَّ عَلٰى آلِ مُحَمَّدٍ وَّ بَارِكْ وَسَلِّمْ عَلٰى مُحَمَّدٍ وَّ عَلٰى

آلِ مُحَمَّدٍ وَّ ارْحَمْ مُحَمَّدًا وَّ آلَ مُحَمَّدٍ كَمَا صَلَّيْتَ وَبَارَكْتَ وَتَرَحَّمْتَ

عَلٰى إِبْرَاهِيْمَ وَعَلٰى آلِ إِبْرَاهِيْمَ فِي الْعَالَمِيْنَ إِنَّكَ حَمِيْدٌ مَّجِيْدٌ

---

139 Si'āya
140 Si'āya

18

اَللّٰهُمَّ صَلِّ عَلٰى مُحَمَّدٍ وَّعَلٰى آلِ مُحَمَّدٍ كَمَا صَلَّيْتَ عَلٰى إِبْرَاهِيمَ وَعَلٰى

آلِ إِبْرَاهِيمَ إِنَّكَ حَمِيدٌ مَّجِيدٌ اَللّٰهُمَّ بَارِكْ عَلٰى مُحَمَّدٍ وَّعَلٰى آلِ مُحَمَّدٍ

كَمَا بَارَكْتَ عَلٰى إِبْرَاهِيمَ وَعَلٰى آلِ إِبْرَاهِيمَ إِنَّكَ حَمِيدٌ مَّجِيدٌ [141]

19

اَللّٰهُمَّ صَلِّ عَلٰى مُحَمَّدٍ عَبْدِكَ وَرَسُوْلِكَ كَمَا صَلَّيْتَ عَلٰى آلِ

إِبْرَاهِيمَ وَبَارِكْ عَلٰى مُحَمَّدٍ وَّعَلٰى آلِ مُحَمَّدٍ كَمَا بَارَكْتَ عَلٰى آلِ

إِبْرَاهِيمَ [142]

20

اَللّٰهُمَّ صَلِّ عَلٰى مُحَمَّدٍ النَّبِيِّ الْأُمِّيِّ وَعَلٰى آلِ مُحَمَّدٍ كَمَا صَلَّيْتَ عَلٰى

إِبْرَاهِيمَ وَبَارِكْ عَلٰى مُحَمَّدٍ النَّبِيِّ الْأُمِّيِّ كَمَا بَارَكْتَ عَلٰى إِبْرَاهِيمَ

إِنَّكَ حَمِيدٌ مَّجِيدٌ [143]

---

141 Sihāh Sitta
142 Nasāi & Ibn Māja
143 Nasāi

21

اَللّٰهُمَّ صَلِّ عَلٰى مُحَمَّدٍ وَّ عَلٰى آلِ مُحَمَّدٍ صَلٰوةً تَكُوْنُ لَكَ رِضًى وَّلِحَقِّهِ

أَدَآءً وَّ أَعْطِهِ الْوَسِيْلَةَ وَالْمَقَامَ الْمَحْمُوْدَ الَّذِيْ وَعَدْتَّهُ وَ اجْزِهِ عَنَّا مَا هُوَ

أَهْلُهُ وَ اجْزِهِ عَنَّا مِنْ أَفْضَلِ مَا جَزَيْتَ نَبِيًّا عَنْ أُمَّتِهِ وَ صَلِّ عَلٰى جَمِيْعِ

إِخْوَانِهِ مِنَ النَّبِيِّيْنَ وَ الصَّالِحِيْنَ يَا أَرْحَمَ الرَّاحِمِيْنَ.[144]

22

اَللّٰهُمَّ صَلِّ عَلٰى مُحَمَّدٍ النَّبِيِّ الْأُمِّيِّ وَعَلٰى آلِ مُحَمَّدٍ كَمَا صَلَّيْتَ عَلٰى

إِبْرَاهِيْمَ وَعَلٰى آلِ إِبْرَاهِيْمَ وَبَارِكْ عَلٰى مُحَمَّدٍ النَّبِيِّ الْأُمِّيِّ وَعَلٰى آلِ

مُحَمَّدٍ كَمَا بَارَكْتَ عَلٰى إِبْرَاهِيْمَ وَعَلٰى آلِ إِبْرَاهِيْمَ إِنَّكَ حَمِيْدٌ مَّجِيْدٌ[145]

23

اَللّٰهُمَّ صَلِّ عَلٰى مُحَمَّدٍ وَّ عَلٰى أَهْلِ بَيْتِهِ كَمَا صَلَّيْتَ عَلٰى إِبْرَاهِيْمَ إِنَّكَ

حَمِيْدٌ مَّجِيْدٌ اَللّٰهُمَّ صَلِّ عَلَيْنَا مَعَهُمْ اَللّٰهُمَّ بَارِكْ عَلٰى مُحَمَّدٍ وَّ عَلٰى أَهْلِ

بَيْتِهِ كَمَا بَارَكْتَ عَلٰى إِبْرَاهِيْمَ إِنَّكَ حَمِيْدٌ مَّجِيْدٌ اَللّٰهُمَّ بَارِكْ عَلَيْنَا

---

144 Ibn Abi 'Āsim 🙼 has narrated that Rasulullah 🙼 said that "whoever read this ṣalāt seven times for seven Jumu'as then my intercession will be incumbent for him." (Al-Qawlul Badi')
145 Bayhaqi, Musnad Aḥmad & Mustadrak Ḥākim

مَعَهُمْ صَلَوَاتُ اللهِ وَصَلَوَاتُ الْمُؤْمِنِيْنَ عَلَى مُحَمَّدٍ النَّبِيِّ الْأُمِّيِّ [146]

24

اَللّٰهُمَّ اجْعَلْ صَلَوَاتِكَ وَبَرَكَاتِكَ عَلَى مُحَمَّدٍ وَّآلِ مُحَمَّدٍ كَمَا جَعَلْتَهَا عَلَى آلِ إِبْرَاهِيْمَ إِنَّكَ حَمِيْدٌ مَّجِيْدٌ وَبَارِكْ عَلَى مُحَمَّدٍ وَّعَلَى آلِ مُحَمَّدٍ كَمَا بَارَكْتَ عَلَى إِبْرَاهِيْمَ وَعَلَى آلِ إِبْرَاهِيْمَ إِنَّكَ حَمِيْدٌ مَّجِيْدٌ [147]

25

وَصَلَّى اللهُ عَلَى النَّبِيِّ الْأُمِّيِّ [148]

146 Dār ul Qutni
147 Ibn Abi 'Āsim
148 Nasāi

137

صيغ السلام

26

ٱلتَّحِيَّاتُ لِلّٰهِ وَالصَّلَوَاتُ وَالطَّيِّبَاتُ ٱلسَّلَامُ عَلَيْكَ أَيُّهَا النَّبِيُّ وَرَحْمَةُ اللّٰهِ وَبَرَكَاتُهُ ٱلسَّلَامُ عَلَيْنَا وَعَلَى عِبَادِ اللّٰهِ الصَّالِحِينَ أَشْهَدُ أَنْ لَاۤ إِلٰهَ إِلَّا اللّٰهُ وَأَشْهَدُ أَنَّ مُحَمَّدًا عَبْدُهُ وَرَسُولُهُ [149]

27

ٱلتَّحِيَّاتُ الطَّيِّبَاتُ الصَّلَوَاتُ لِلّٰهِ ٱلسَّلَامُ عَلَيْكَ أَيُّهَا النَّبِيُّ وَرَحْمَةُ اللّٰهِ وَبَرَكَاتُهُ ٱلسَّلَامُ عَلَيْنَا وَعَلَى عِبَادِ اللّٰهِ الصَّالِحِينَ أَشْهَدُ أَنْ لَاۤ إِلٰهَ إِلَّا اللّٰهُ وَأَشْهَدُ أَنَّ مُحَمَّدًا عَبْدُهُ وَرَسُولُهُ.

28

ٱلتَّحِيَّاتُ لِلّٰهِ الطَّيِّبَاتُ الصَّلَوَاتُ لِلّٰهِ ٱلسَّلَامُ عَلَيْكَ أَيُّهَا النَّبِيُّ وَرَحْمَةُ اللّٰهِ وَبَرَكَاتُهُ ٱلسَّلَامُ عَلَيْنَا وَعَلَى عِبَادِ اللّٰهِ الصَّالِحِينَ أَشْهَدُ أَنْ لَاۤ إِلٰهَ إِلَّا اللّٰهُ وَحْدَهُ لَاشَرِيكَ لَهُ وَأَشْهَدُ أَنَّ مُحَمَّدًا عَبْدُهُ وَرَسُولُهُ [151]

---

149 Bukhāri Sharīf & Nasāi
150 Nasāi & Muslim
151 Nasāi

29

اَلتَّحِيَّاتُ الْمُبَارَكَاتُ الصَّلَوَاتُ الطَّيِّبَاتُ لِلّٰهِ سَلَامٌ عَلَيْكَ أَيُّهَا النَّبِيُّ وَرَحْمَةُ اللّٰهِ وَبَرَكَاتُهُ سَلَامٌ عَلَيْنَا وَعَلَى عِبَادِ اللّٰهِ الصَّالِحِينَ أَشْهَدُ أَنْ لَّا إِلٰهَ إِلَّا اللّٰهُ وَأَشْهَدُ أَنَّ مُحَمَّدًا عَبْدُهُ وَرَسُولُهُ١٥٢

30

بِسْمِ اللّٰهِ وَبِاللّٰهِ اَلتَّحِيَّاتُ لِلّٰهِ وَالصَّلَوَاتُ وَالطَّيِّبَاتُ اَلسَّلَامُ عَلَيْكَ أَيُّهَا النَّبِيُّ وَرَحْمَةُ اللّٰهِ وَبَرَكَاتُهُ اَلسَّلَامُ عَلَيْنَا وَعَلَى عِبَادِ اللّٰهِ الصَّالِحِينَ أَشْهَدُ أَنْ لَّا إِلٰهَ إِلَّا اللّٰهُ وَأَشْهَدُ أَنَّ مُحَمَّدًا عَبْدُهُ وَرَسُولُهُ أَسْأَلُ اللّٰهَ الْجَنَّةَ وَأَعُوذُ بِاللّٰهِ مِنَ النَّارِ١٥٣

31

اَلتَّحِيَّاتُ الزَّاكِيَاتُ لِلّٰهِ الطَّيِّبَاتُ الصَّلَوَاتُ لِلّٰهِ اَلسَّلَامُ عَلَيْكَ أَيُّهَا النَّبِيُّ وَرَحْمَةُ اللّٰهِ وَبَرَكَاتُهُ اَلسَّلَامُ عَلَيْنَا وَعَلَى عِبَادِ اللّٰهِ الصَّالِحِينَ أَشْهَدُ أَنْ لَّا إِلٰهَ إِلَّا اللّٰهُ وَأَشْهَدُ أَنَّ مُحَمَّدًا عَبْدُهُ وَرَسُولُهُ١٥٤

---

152 Nasāī
153 Nasāī
154 Muwatta

32

بِسْمِ اللهِ وَبِاللهِ خَيْرِ الْأَسْمَاءِ اَلتَّحِيَّاتُ الطَّيِّبَاتُ الصَّلَوَاتُ لِلهِ أَشْهَدُ

أَنْ لَّا إِلهَ إِلَّا اللهُ وَحْدَهُ لَا شَرِيكَ لَهُ وَأَشْهَدُ أَنَّ مُحَمَّدًا عَبْدُهُ وَرَسُولُهُ

أَرْسَلَهُ بِالْحَقِّ بَشِيرًا وَنَذِيرًا وَأَنَّ السَّاعَةَ آتِيَةٌ لَّا رَيْبَ فِيهَا اَلسَّلامُ

عَلَيْكَ أَيُّهَا النَّبِيُّ وَرَحْمَةُ اللهِ وَبَرَكَاتُهُ اَلسَّلامُ عَلَيْنَا وَعَلَى عِبَادِ اللهِ

الصَّالِحِينَ اَللَّهُمَّ اغْفِرْ لِي وَاهْدِنِي [155]

33

اَلتَّحِيَّاتُ الطَّيِّبَاتُ وَالصَّلَوَاتُ وَالْمُلْكُ لِلهِ اَلسَّلامُ عَلَيْكَ أَيُّهَا النَّبِيُّ

وَرَحْمَةُ اللهِ وَبَرَكَاتُهُ [156]

34

بِسْمِ اللهِ اَلتَّحِيَّاتُ لِلهِ الصَّلَوَاتُ لِلهِ الزَّاكِيَاتُ لِلهِ اَلسَّلامُ عَلَى النَّبِيِّ

وَرَحْمَةُ اللهِ وَبَرَكَاتُهُ اَلسَّلامُ عَلَيْنَا وَعَلَى عِبَادِ اللهِ الصَّالِحِينَ شَهِدْتُّ

أَنْ لَّا إِلهَ إِلَّا اللهُ شَهِدْتُّ أَنَّ مُحَمَّدًا رَسُولُ اللهِ [157]

---

155 Mu'jam Tabarāni
156 Abu Dawūd
157 Muwatta

35

اَلتَّحِيَّاتُ الطَّيِّبَاتُ الصَّلَوَاتُ الزَّاكِيَاتُ لِلهِ أَشْهَدُ أَنْ لاَّ إِلهَ إِلاَّ اللهُ

وَحْدَهُ لَا شَرِيْكَ لَهُ وَأَنَّ مُحَمَّدًا عَبْدُهُ وَرَسُوْلُهُ اَلسَّلَامُ عَلَيْكَ أَيُّهَا

النَّبِيُّ وَرَحْمَةُ اللهِ وَبَرَكَاتُهُ اَلسَّلَامُ عَلَيْنَا وَعَلَى عِبَادِ اللهِ الصَّالِحِيْنَ[158]

36

اَلتَّحِيَّاتُ الطَّيِّبَاتُ الصَّلَوَاتُ الزَّاكِيَاتُ لِلهِ أَشْهَدُ أَنْ لاَّ إِلهَ إِلاَّ اللهُ

وَأَشْهَدُ أَنَّ مُحَمَّدًا عَبْدُ اللهِ وَرَسُوْلُهُ اَلسَّلَامُ عَلَيْكَ أَيُّهَا النَّبِيُّ

وَرَحْمَةُ اللهِ وَبَرَكَاتُهُ اَلسَّلَامُ عَلَيْنَا وَعَلَى عِبَادِ اللهِ الصَّالِحِيْنَ[159]

37

اَلتَّحِيَّاتُ الصَّلَوَاتُ لِلهِ اَلسَّلَامُ عَلَيْكَ أَيُّهَا النَّبِيُّ وَرَحْمَةُ اللهِ

وَبَرَكَاتُهُ اَلسَّلَامُ عَلَيْنَا وَعَلَى عِبَادِ اللهِ الصَّالِحِيْنَ

38

اَلتَّحِيَّاتُ لِلهِ الصَّلَوَاتُ الطَّيِّبَاتُ اَلسَّلَامُ عَلَيْكَ أَيُّهَا النَّبِيُّ وَرَحْمَةُ

اللهِ اَلسَّلَامُ عَلَيْنَا وَعَلَى عِبَادِ اللهِ الصَّالِحِيْنَ أَشْهَدُ أَنْ لاَّ إِلهَ إِلاَّ اللهُ

---

158 Muwatta
159 Muwatta
160 Taḥāwi

141

وَأَشْهَدُ أَنَّ مُحَمَّدًا عَبْدُهُ وَرَسُوْلُهُ[161]

39

اَلتَّحِيَّاتُ الْمُبَارَكَاتُ الصَّلَوَاتُ الطَّيِّبَاتُ لِلهِ اَلسَّلَامُ عَلَيْكَ أَيُّهَا النَّبِيُّ وَرَحْمَةُ اللهِ وَبَرَكَاتُهُ اَلسَّلَامُ عَلَيْنَا وَعَلَى عِبَادِ اللهِ الصَّالِحِينَ أَشْهَدُ أَنْ لَّا إِلَهَ إِلَّا اللهُ وَأَشْهَدُ أَنَّ مُحَمَّدًا رَسُوْلُ اللهِ[162]

40

بِسْمِ اللهِ وَالسَّلَامُ عَلَى رَسُوْلِ اللهِ[163]

---

161 Abu Dawūd
162 Muslim Sharīf
163 Mustadrak Ḥākim

Verses from the Holy Qurān to protect from mischief, sorcery and other harms.

Manzil

This compilation also contains notes on the virtues and blessings of the compiled holy verses. The notes are concise, so while reading, it will create enthusiasm and spiritual benefits as well.

This is a collection of verses from the Qurān. In my family this was known as *Manzil*. The elders of my family used to be very particular in using these verses in du'ās and treatments. The children of our family were made to memorise the Manzil at a young age.

In place of amulets (that are permissible according to shari'a), the veres of Qurān and those du'ās that are in the aḥādīth are much more effective and beneficial. When treating people one should be mindful of this.

Rasulullāh ﷺ did not leave out any need of this world or the hereafter except that he taught a du'ā by means of which to resolve that need. Experience has shown that there are certain verses when read while in a specific need or difficulty, Allāh will alleviate that need or difficulty.

Manzil is a tried and tested practice for protection and cure from mischief, siḥr and other harmful things. These verses are compiled in al-Qawlul Jamīl and Beheshti Zewar. In al-Qawlul Jamīl, Shah Waliullah Muḥaddith Dehlawi ﷲ‎ has stated that "there are thirty-three verses that remove the effects of black magic and protect from shaytāns, thieves and wild animals". In Beheshti Zewar, Mawlāna Ashraf Thānwi ﷲ‎ has said written that "that whoever is fearful that that someone is afflicted, they should have these verses written and hung on the person's neck or that these verses can be recited and then the reader blow on some water and that water is sprinkled on the patient or that the water is sprinkled in the four corners of the house."

In our family, it was quite difficult for the ladies to read these verses for anybody that was sick or afflicted as they had to go through the Qurān and find the verses which were usually book marked. Therefore, to make things easy, a separate compilation was prepared.

Treatments and duʿās are effective according to the manner they are recited. The more concentration, focus and love that duʿās are read with, the more effective they become. There are great blessings in the name and kalām of Allāh.

Ḥaḍrat Mawlāna Muḥammad Talha al-Kandahlawi son of Ḥaḍrat Shaykh Mawlāna Muḥammad Zakariyya Sāhib رحمه الله.

22nd Shaban 1399 Hijri

Important Note

1. Within the footnotes there are virtues and blessings (from āhadīth) of the verses of the Manzil. By reading these, enthusiasm will be created. Therefore, every now and then these should also be read. However, they are not part of the actual Manzil.
2. The Manzil can be held without wuḍu but the reader should be mindful not to touch the verses when handling the book while not in a state of wuḍu. This ruling does not apply to handling a Qurān i.e. you can not handle a Qurān without wuḍu.

بِسْمِ اللهِ الرَّحْمٰنِ الرَّحِيمِ

اَلْحَمْدُ لِلّٰهِ رَبِّ الْعٰلَمِينَ ﴿١﴾ اَلرَّحْمٰنِ الرَّحِيمِ ﴿٢﴾ مٰلِكِ يَوْمِ الدِّينِ ﴿٣﴾ إِيَّاكَ نَعْبُدُ وَإِيَّاكَ نَسْتَعِينُ ﴿٤﴾ اِهْدِنَا الصِّرَاطَ الْمُسْتَقِيمَ ﴿٥﴾ صِرَاطَ الَّذِينَ أَنْعَمْتَ عَلَيْهِمْ غَيْرِ الْمَغْضُوبِ عَلَيْهِمْ وَلَا الضَّالِّينَ ﴿٦﴾[١٦٤]

بِسْمِ اللهِ الرَّحْمٰنِ الرَّحِيمِ

الٓمٓ ﴿١﴾ ذٰلِكَ الْكِتَابُ لَا رَيْبَ فِيهِ هُدًى لِّلْمُتَّقِينَ ﴿٢﴾ الَّذِينَ يُؤْمِنُونَ بِالْغَيْبِ وَيُقِيمُونَ الصَّلٰوةَ وَمِمَّا رَزَقْنٰهُمْ يُنْفِقُونَ ﴿٣﴾ وَالَّذِينَ يُؤْمِنُونَ بِمَا أُنْزِلَ إِلَيْكَ وَمَا أُنْزِلَ مِنْ قَبْلِكَ وَبِالْآخِرَةِ هُمْ يُوقِنُونَ ﴿٤﴾ أُولٰئِكَ عَلَىٰ هُدًى مِّنْ رَّبِّهِمْ وَأُولٰئِكَ هُمُ الْمُفْلِحُونَ ﴿٥﴾[١٦٥]

---

164 In a ḥadīth it is narrated from Rasulullah ﷺ that Sura Fātiḥa is cure for all ailments (Dārimi and Baihaqi). In it is also encouraged in another ḥadīth to read it and blow on the patient.

165 It is narrated in a ḥadīth by Ḥaḍrat 'Abdullah ibn Mas'ood ؓ that there are ten verses in Sura Baqara that have such an efficacy that if one recites them at night, neither Shayṭān nor the jinn would enter one's house, nor would one and one's family be afflicted with illness or calamity or sorrow that night, and that if they are recited over a man suffering from a fit of madness, his condition will improve. The ten verses are these: the first four verses of the Sura, three verses in the middle (that is, the Āyāt al Kursi, and the two following verses), and the last three verses of the Sura. (Ma'āriful Qurān)

146

وَاِلٰهُكُمْ اِلٰهٌ وَّاحِدٌ ۖ لَّا اِلٰهَ اِلَّا هُوَ الرَّحْمٰنُ الرَّحِيْمُ ۞١١٣ ۞١٦٦

اَللّٰهُ لَا اِلٰهَ اِلَّا هُوَ الْحَيُّ الْقَيُّوْمُ ۚ لَا تَأْخُذُهٗ سِنَةٌ وَّلَا نَوْمٌ ۚ لَهٗ مَا فِي السَّمٰوٰتِ وَ مَا فِي الْاَرْضِ ۗ مَنْ ذَا الَّذِيْ يَشْفَعُ عِنْدَهٗٓ اِلَّا بِاِذْنِهٖ ۚ يَعْلَمُ مَا بَيْنَ اَيْدِيْهِمْ وَ مَا خَلْفَهُمْ ۚ وَ لَا يُحِيْطُوْنَ بِشَيْءٍ مِّنْ عِلْمِهٖٓ اِلَّا بِمَا شَاءَ ۚ وَسِعَ كُرْسِيُّهُ السَّمٰوٰتِ وَ الْاَرْضَ ۚ وَ لَا يَئُوْدُهٗ حِفْظُهُمَا ۚ وَ هُوَ الْعَلِيُّ الْعَظِيْمُ ۞٢٥٥ لَا اِكْرَاهَ فِي الدِّيْنِ ۟ قَدْ تَّبَيَّنَ الرُّشْدُ مِنَ الْغَيِّ ۚ فَمَنْ يَّكْفُرْ بِالطَّاغُوْتِ وَ يُؤْمِنْ بِاللّٰهِ فَقَدِ اسْتَمْسَكَ بِالْعُرْوَةِ الْوُثْقٰى لَا انْفِصَامَ لَهَا ۗ وَ اللّٰهُ سَمِيْعٌ عَلِيْمٌ ۞٢٥٦ اَللّٰهُ وَلِيُّ الَّذِيْنَ اٰمَنُوْا ۙ يُخْرِجُهُمْ مِّنَ الظُّلُمٰتِ اِلَى النُّوْرِ ۚ وَ الَّذِيْنَ كَفَرُوْٓا اَوْلِيٰٓئُهُمُ الطَّاغُوْتُ ۙ يُخْرِجُوْنَهُمْ مِّنَ النُّوْرِ اِلَى الظُّلُمٰتِ ۗ اُولٰٓئِكَ اَصْحٰبُ النَّارِ ۚ هُمْ فِيْهَا خٰلِدُوْنَ ۞٢٥٧

لِلّٰهِ مَا فِي السَّمٰوٰتِ وَ مَا فِي الْاَرْضِ ۗ وَ اِنْ تُبْدُوْا مَا فِيْٓ اَنْفُسِكُمْ اَوْ تُخْفُوْهُ يُحَاسِبْكُمْ بِهِ اللّٰهُ ۖ فَيَغْفِرُ لِمَنْ يَّشَاءُ وَ يُعَذِّبُ مَنْ يَّشَاءُ ۗ وَ اللّٰهُ عَلٰى كُلِّ

---

166 This verse is pure tawheed, upon which all of dīn depends.

147

شَىْءٍ قَدِيْرٌ ﴿٢٨٣﴾ ءَامَنَ الرَّسُوْلُ بِمَاۤ أُنْزِلَ إِلَيْهِ مِنْ رَّبِّهٖ وَالْمُؤْمِنُوْنَ كُلٌّ

ءَامَنَ بِاللّٰهِ وَمَلٰٓئِكَتِهٖ وَكُتُبِهٖ وَرُسُلِهٖ لَا نُفَرِّقُ بَيْنَ أَحَدٍ مِّنْ رُّسُلِهٖ وَ

قَالُوْا سَمِعْنَا وَأَطَعْنَا غُفْرَانَكَ رَبَّنَا وَإِلَيْكَ الْمَصِيْرُ ﴿٢٨٥﴾ لَا يُكَلِّفُ اللّٰهُ

نَفْسًا إِلَّا وُسْعَهَا لَهَا مَا كَسَبَتْ وَعَلَيْهَا مَا اكْتَسَبَتْ رَبَّنَا لَا تُؤَاخِذْنَاۤ إِنْ

نَّسِيْنَاۤ أَوْ أَخْطَأْنَا رَبَّنَا وَلَا تَحْمِلْ عَلَيْنَاۤ إِصْرًا كَمَا حَمَلْتَهٗ عَلَى الَّذِيْنَ مِنْ

قَبْلِنَا رَبَّنَا وَلَا تُحَمِّلْنَا مَا لَا طَاقَةَ لَنَا بِهٖ وَاعْفُ عَنَّا وَاغْفِرْ لَنَا وَ

ارْحَمْنَا أَنْتَ مَوْلٰىنَا فَانْصُرْنَا عَلَى الْقَوْمِ الْكٰفِرِيْنَ ﴿٢٨٦﴾ ١٦٧

شَهِدَ اللّٰهُ أَنَّهٗ لَاۤ إِلٰهَ إِلَّا هُوَ وَالْمَلٰٓئِكَةُ وَأُولُوا الْعِلْمِ قَآئِمًا بِالْقِسْطِ لَاۤ إِلٰهَ

إِلَّا هُوَ الْعَزِيْزُ الْحَكِيْمُ ﴿١٨﴾ ١٦٨

قُلِ اللّٰهُمَّ مٰلِكَ الْمُلْكِ تُؤْتِي الْمُلْكَ مَنْ تَشَآءُ وَتَنْزِعُ الْمُلْكَ مِمَّنْ تَشَآءُ

167 In a ḥadīth it is mentioned that Rasulullah ﷺ has said that Allāh ﷻ has ended sura Baqara with these two verses which are a treasure specially given to me from below the A'rsh. Therefore, be particular in learning them and also teach them to your womenfolk and children. (Mustadrak Ḥākim, Bayhaqī)
168 Ḥaḍrat Abu Ayūb al-Anṣāri ؓ narrated a ḥadīth in which the Prophet ﷺ said that whoever reads after the Farḍ prayers Ayātul Kursi and the verse شَهِدَ اللّٰهُ and قُلِ اللّٰهُمَّ مٰلِكَ الْمُلْكِ until يَغَيِّر حِسَاب, Allāh will forgive his sins and place him in Paradise and fulfil seventy of his needs, the least of which is that he will attain forgiveness. (Rūhul Ma'āni).

148

وَتُعِزُّ مَنْ تَشَآءُ وَتُذِلُّ مَنْ تَشَآءُ بِيَدِكَ الْخَيْرُ إِنَّكَ عَلَى كُلِّ شَىْءٍ

قَدِيرٌ ۝ تُوْلِجُ الَّيْلَ فِي النَّهَارِ وَتُوْلِجُ النَّهَارَ فِي الَّيْلِ وَتُخْرِجُ الْحَىَّ مِنَ

الْمَيِّتِ وَتُخْرِجُ الْمَيِّتَ مِنَ الْحَىِّ وَتَرْزُقُ مَنْ تَشَآءُ بِغَيْرِ حِسَابٍ ۝

إِنَّ رَبَّكُمُ اللهُ الَّذِى خَلَقَ السَّمٰوٰتِ وَالْأَرْضَ فِي سِتَّةِ أَيَّامٍ ثُمَّ اسْتَوٰى

عَلَى الْعَرْشِ يُغْشِى الَّيْلَ النَّهَارَ يَطْلُبُهُ حَثِيثًا وَّالشَّمْسَ وَالْقَمَرَ وَ

النُّجُوْمَ مُسَخَّرٰتٍ بِأَمْرِهِ أَلَا لَهُ الْخَلْقُ وَالْأَمْرُ تَبٰرَكَ اللهُ رَبُّ

الْعٰلَمِيْنَ ۝ اُدْعُوْا رَبَّكُمْ تَضَرُّعًا وَّخُفْيَةً إِنَّهُ لَا يُحِبُّ

الْمُعْتَدِيْنَ ۝ وَلَا تُفْسِدُوْا فِي الْأَرْضِ بَعْدَ إِصْلَاحِهَا وَادْعُوْهُ خَوْفًا وَّ

طَمَعًا إِنَّ رَحْمَتَ اللهِ قَرِيْبٌ مِّنَ الْمُحْسِنِيْنَ ۝ ¹⁶⁹

قُلِ ادْعُوا اللهَ أَوِ ادْعُوا الرَّحْمٰنَ أَيًّا مَّا تَدْعُوْا فَلَهُ الْأَسْمَآءُ الْحُسْنٰى وَلَا

تَجْهَرْ بِصَلَاتِكَ وَلَا تُخَافِتْ بِهَا وَابْتَغِ بَيْنَ ذٰلِكَ سَبِيْلًا ۝ وَقُلِ

---

169 These three verses of the Holy Qurān are well known for being effective in repelling harm.

الْحَمْدُ لِلّٰهِ الَّذِىْ لَمْ يَتَّخِذْ وَلَدًا وَّلَمْ يَكُنْ لَّهُ شَرِيْكٌ فِى الْمُلْكِ وَلَمْ

يَكُنْ لَّهُ وَلِيٌّ مِّنَ الذُّلِّ وَ كَبِّرْهُ تَكْبِيْرًا ﴿١١١﴾ ١٧٠

اَفَحَسِبْتُمْ اَنَّمَا خَلَقْنٰكُمْ عَبَثًا وَّاَنَّكُمْ اِلَيْنَا لَا تُرْجَعُوْنَ ﴿١١٥﴾ فَتَعٰلَى

اللّٰهُ الْمَلِكُ الْحَقُّ لَا اِلٰهَ اِلَّا هُوَ رَبُّ الْعَرْشِ الْكَرِيْمِ ﴿١١٦﴾ وَمَنْ يَّدْعُ

مَعَ اللّٰهِ اِلٰهًا اٰخَرَ لَا بُرْهَانَ لَهُ بِهِ فَاِنَّمَا حِسَابُهُ عِنْدَ رَبِّهِ اِنَّهُ لَا يُفْلِحُ

الْكٰفِرُوْنَ ﴿١١٧﴾ وَقُلْ رَّبِّ اغْفِرْ وَارْحَمْ وَاَنْتَ خَيْرُ الرّٰحِمِيْنَ

﴿١١٨ ١٧١﴾

بِسْمِ اللّٰهِ الرَّحْمٰنِ الرَّحِيْمِ

وَ الصّٰٓفّٰتِ صَفًّا ﴿١﴾ فَالزّٰجِرٰتِ زَجْرًا ﴿٢﴾ فَالتّٰلِيٰتِ ذِكْرًا ﴿٣﴾ اِنَّ

اِلٰهَكُمْ لَوَاحِدٌ ﴿٤﴾ رَبُّ السَّمٰوٰتِ وَالْاَرْضِ وَمَا بَيْنَهُمَا وَرَبُّ

الْمَشَارِقِ ﴿٥﴾ اِنَّا زَيَّنَّا السَّمَآءَ الدُّنْيَا بِزِيْنَةِ الْكَوَاكِبِ ﴿٦﴾ وَ

---

170 Hadhrat Abu Musa Ashari ؓ has narrated that Rasulullah ﷺ said that whoever recites these verses in the morning or evening till the end of the sura, his heart will not die on that day or night. (Daylami)
171 Haḍrat Muḥammad Bin Ibrāhīm Taymi narrated from his father that he was sent by Rasulullah ﷺ in one expedition. At the time of departure Rasulullah ﷺ advised him that they should read these verses morning and evening. We used to read these by means of which we obtained much wealth (spoils of war) and our lives were also protected. (Ibn us Sunni)

150

حِفْظًا مِّنْ كُلِّ شَيْطٰنٍ مَّارِدٍ ۞ لَّا يَسَّمَّعُوۡنَ إِلَى الْمَلَإِ الْأَعْلٰى وَيُقْذَفُوۡنَ مِنْ كُلِّ جَانِبٍ ۞ دُحُوۡرًا وَّلَهُمْ عَذَابٌ وَّاصِبٌ ۞ إِلَّا مَنْ خَطِفَ الْخَطْفَةَ فَأَتْبَعَهُ شِهَابٌ ثَاقِبٌ ۞ فَاسْتَفْتِهِمْ أَهُمْ أَشَدُّ خَلْقًا أَمْ مَّنْ خَلَقْنَا ۚ إِنَّا خَلَقْنٰهُمْ مِّنْ طِيْنٍ لَّازِبٍ ۞

يٰمَعْشَرَ الْجِنِّ وَالْإِنْسِ إِنِ اسْتَطَعْتُمْ أَنْ تَنْفُذُوۡا مِنْ أَقْطَارِ السَّمٰوٰتِ وَالْأَرْضِ فَانْفُذُوۡا ۚ لَا تَنْفُذُوۡنَ إِلَّا بِسُلْطٰنٍ ۞ فَبِأَيِّ آلَاءِ رَبِّكُمَا تُكَذِّبٰنِ ۞ يُرْسَلُ عَلَيْكُمَا شُوَاظٌ مِّنْ نَّارٍ وَّنُحَاسٌ فَلَا تَنْتَصِرَانِ ۞ فَبِأَيِّ آلَاءِ رَبِّكُمَا تُكَذِّبٰنِ ۞ فَإِذَا انْشَقَّتِ السَّمَآءُ فَكَانَتْ وَرْدَةً كَالدِّهَانِ ۞ فَبِأَيِّ آلَاءِ رَبِّكُمَا تُكَذِّبٰنِ ۞ فَيَوْمَئِذٍ لَّا يُسْأَلُ عَنْ ذَنْبِهٖ إِنْسٌ وَّلَا جَآنٌّ ۞ فَبِأَيِّ آلَاءِ رَبِّكُمَا تُكَذِّبٰنِ

۞ ۱۷۲ ۞

---

172 These verses of the Holy Qurān are well known for being effective in repelling harm.

لَوْ أَنْزَلْنَا هٰذَا الْقُرْآنَ عَلٰى جَبَلٍ لَّرَأَيْتَهٗ خَاشِعًا مُّتَصَدِّعًا مِّنْ خَشْيَةِ اللهِ ۚ

وَتِلْكَ الْأَمْثَالُ نَضْرِبُهَا لِلنَّاسِ لَعَلَّهُمْ يَتَفَكَّرُوْنَ ﴿﴾ هُوَ اللهُ الَّذِيْ لَا

إِلٰهَ إِلَّا هُوَ ۚ عٰلِمُ الْغَيْبِ وَالشَّهَادَةِ ۚ هُوَ الرَّحْمٰنُ الرَّحِيْمُ ﴿﴾ هُوَ اللهُ

الَّذِيْ لَا إِلٰهَ إِلَّا هُوَ ۚ الْمَلِكُ الْقُدُّوْسُ السَّلٰمُ الْمُؤْمِنُ الْمُهَيْمِنُ الْعَزِيْزُ

الْجَبَّارُ الْمُتَكَبِّرُ ۚ سُبْحٰنَ اللهِ عَمَّا يُشْرِكُوْنَ ﴿﴾ هُوَ اللهُ الْخَالِقُ الْبَارِئُ

الْمُصَوِّرُ لَهُ الْأَسْمَاءُ الْحُسْنٰى ۚ يُسَبِّحُ لَهٗ مَا فِي السَّمٰوٰتِ وَالْأَرْضِ ۚ وَهُوَ

الْعَزِيْزُ الْحَكِيْمُ ﴿١٧٣﴾

بِسْمِ اللهِ الرَّحْمٰنِ الرَّحِيْمِ

قُلْ أُوْحِيَ إِلَيَّ أَنَّهُ اسْتَمَعَ نَفَرٌ مِّنَ الْجِنِّ فَقَالُوْا إِنَّا سَمِعْنَا قُرْآنًا عَجَبًا ﴿﴾

يَّهْدِيْ إِلَى الرُّشْدِ فَآمَنَّا بِهٖ ۚ وَلَنْ نُّشْرِكَ بِرَبِّنَا أَحَدًا ﴿﴾ وَّأَنَّهُ تَعٰلٰى جَدُّ

بَنَامَا اتَّخَذَ صَاحِبَةً وَّلَا وَلَدًا ۞ وَّاَنَّهُ كَانَ يَقُوْلُ سَفِيْهُنَا عَلَى اللهِ

شَطَطًا ۞١٧٤

بِسْمِ اللهِ الرَّحْمٰنِ الرَّحِيْمِ

قُلْ يٰٓاَيُّهَا الْكٰفِرُوْنَ ۞ لَآ اَعْبُدُ مَا تَعْبُدُوْنَ ۞ وَلَآ اَنْتُمْ عٰبِدُوْنَ

مَآ اَعْبُدُ ۞ وَلَآ اَنَا عَابِدٌ مَّا عَبَدتُّمْ ۞ وَلَآ اَنْتُمْ عٰبِدُوْنَ مَآ اَعْبُدُ

۞ لَكُمْ دِيْنُكُمْ وَلِيَ دِيْنِ ۞١٧٥

بِسْمِ اللهِ الرَّحْمٰنِ الرَّحِيْمِ

قُلْ هُوَ اللهُ اَحَدٌ ۞ اَللهُ الصَّمَدُ ۞ لَمْ يَلِدْ وَلَمْ يُوْلَدْ ۞ وَلَمْ

يَكُنْ لَّهُ كُفُوًا اَحَدٌ ۞١٧٦

---

174 These verses of Qurān are well known for being effective in repelling harm.
175 Ḥaḍrat Jubayr Bin Mut'im ⬟ narrates from the holy Prophet ⬟ says that he asked him whether he wished to have the best companions and the most amount of provisions with him when he was on a journey, and he said he definitely wanted that, then, the Prophet ⬟ said: "Recite these five Surahs: Sura Kafirūn, Sura Nasr, Sura Ikhlās, Sura Falaq and Sura Nās, and begin your recitation (of each sura) with Bismillah and end (the sura Nās) with Bismillah. (Tafsīr Maẓhari) It is narrated that Sura Kafirūn is equal to one fourth of the Qurān. (Tirmidhi)
176 In one narration, Sura Ikhlās is equated to one third of the Qurān.

بِسْمِ اللهِ الرَّحْمٰنِ الرَّحِيْمِ

قُلْ اَعُوْذُ بِرَبِّ الْفَلَقِ ۞ مِنْ شَرِّ مَا خَلَقَ ۞ وَمِنْ شَرِّ غَاسِقٍ اِذَا

وَقَبَ ۞ وَمِنْ شَرِّ النَّفّٰثٰتِ فِى الْعُقَدِ ۞ وَمِنْ شَرِّ حَاسِدٍ اِذَا حَسَدَ

۞ 177 ۞

بِسْمِ اللهِ الرَّحْمٰنِ الرَّحِيْمِ

قُلْ اَعُوْذُ بِرَبِّ النَّاسِ ۞ مَلِكِ النَّاسِ ۞ اِلٰهِ النَّاسِ

۞ مِنْ شَرِّ الْوَسْوَاسِ الْخَنَّاسِ ۞ الَّذِىْ يُوَسْوِسُ فِىْ صُدُوْرِ النَّاسِ

۞ مِنَ الْجِنَّةِ وَ النَّاسِ ۞

---

177 In a lengthy ḥadīth it is narrated that Rasulullah ﷺ said that that whoever reads قُلْ هُوَ اللهُ اَحَدٌ and the Mu'awwadhtayn (Sura Falaq and Sura Nās) that it will suffice him. In another narration it will suffice him in protecting him from all calamaties. Imam has narrated from Haḍrat 'Uqba ibn 'Āmir ؓ that Rasulullah ﷺ said that I shall tell you of three suras that were revealed in the Taurāt, Zabūr, Injīl and the Qurān. Don't sleep at night until you have recited these three (i.e. قُلْ هُوَ اللهُ اَحَدٌ and the Mu'awwadhtayn). Haḍrat Uqba ؓ said since that time I never missed reading these suras (Musnad Aḥmad).

وَلِلّٰهِ الْأَسْمَاءُ الْحُسْنَى فَادْعُوهُ بِهَا

هُوَ اللّٰهُ الَّذِي لَا إِلٰهَ إِلَّا هُوَ

السَّلَامُ	الْقُدُّوسُ	الْمَلِكُ	الرَّحِيمُ	الرَّحْمٰنُ
الْمُتَكَبِّرُ	الْجَبَّارُ	الْعَزِيزُ	الْمُهَيْمِنُ	الْمُؤْمِنُ
الْقَهَّارُ	الْغَفَّارُ	الْمُصَوِّرُ	الْبَارِئُ	الْخَالِقُ
الْقَابِضُ	الْعَلِيمُ	الْفَتَّاحُ	الرَّزَّاقُ	الْوَهَّابُ
الْمُذِلُّ	الْمُعِزُّ	الرَّافِعُ	الْخَافِضُ	الْبَاسِطُ
اللَّطِيفُ	الْعَدْلُ	الْحَكَمُ	الْبَصِيرُ	السَّمِيعُ
الشَّكُورُ	الْغَفُورُ	الْعَظِيمُ	الْحَلِيمُ	الْخَبِيرُ
الْحَسِيبُ	الْمُقِيتُ	الْحَفِيظُ	الْكَبِيرُ	الْعَلِيُّ
الْوَاسِعُ	الْمُجِيبُ	الرَّقِيبُ	الْكَرِيمُ	الْجَلِيلُ
الشَّهِيدُ	الْبَاعِثُ	الْمَجِيدُ	الْوَدُودُ	الْحَكِيمُ

155

الوَلِيُّ	المَتِينُ	القَوِيُّ	الوَكِيلُ	الحَقُّ
المُحْيِي	المُعِيدُ	المُبْدِئُ	المُحْصِي	الحَمِيدُ
المَاجِدُ	الوَاجِدُ	القَيُّومُ	الحَيُّ	المُمِيتُ
المُقَدِّمُ	المُقْتَدِرُ	القَادِرُ	الصَّمَدُ	الوَاحِدُ
البَاطِنُ	الظَّاهِرُ	الآخِرُ	الأَوَّلُ	المُؤَخِّرُ
المُنْتَقِمُ	التَّوَّابُ	البَرُّ	المُتَعَالِ	الوَالِي
ذُو الجَلَالِ	المَلِكِ مَالِكُ	الرَّءُوفُ	العَفُوُّ
المُغْنِي	الغَنِيُّ	الجَامِعُ	المُقْسِطُ	وَالإِكْرَامِ
الهَادِي	النُّورُ	النَّافِعُ	الضَّارُّ	المَانِعُ
الصَّبُورُ	الرَّشِيدُ	الوَارِثُ	البَاقِي	البَدِيعُ

الطَّرِيْقُ لِمَنْ فَقَدَ الرَّفِيْق

The Path for the one who has lost his travelling companion

Our murshid (guide) the noble Sheikh ul Ḥadīth Ḥaḍrat Mawlāna Muḥammad Zakariyya رَحِمَهُ اللّٰه said that reciting, reading to others and disseminating ṣalawāt is a definite means of achieving the good of both worlds and nearness to Allāh. That is why I always advise my friends to remember death and recite the ṣalawāt as much as they can.

About remembrance of death and ṣalawāt

To have a connection or attachment to Allāh, purification is essential i.e. to remove blameworthy traits and to acquire praiseworthy ones. For this, a relationship of baiʿa (pledge) and iṣlāḥ (rectification) needs to be established with a sheikh of tariqa who follows the Sunna. The path of tariqa requires two things muḥabba (love) and suḥba (companionship) of a sheikh kāmil (accomplished) and there afterwards to make abundant dhikr in the sheikh's supervision. However, as we live in a time of evil and vice and we are unable to find a sheikh that we can have affinity with then for such a person the mashāikh have prescribed an easy way to to achieve iḥsān. They still need to go to through the first step of baiʿa which is to to make their beliefs in accordance to the Ahlus Sunna Wal Jamaʿa, then they must learn the knowledge of the pillars of Islām, the farāiḍ (obligatory aspects of Islamic law) and those things that are forbidden. Then

157

he would also have to act according as well. For this studying "Beheshti Zewar"[178] with a reliable ʿālim is sufficient.

This person should also remember death much and should do istighfār and tawba. By remembering death often, high expectations on dunya will end and the love of dunya will come out of his heart. The love of dunya is the root of all vice. For this reason, the reading of the booklet *Remembrance of Death* will be beneficial.

The next step would be to create a connection and attachment to Allāh by making abundant dhikr in accordance to a tariqa. But this must happen under the supervision of a sheikh, so that whenever some condition comes over the sālik (seeker) then the sheikh can advice and guide him.

It is observed that the ṣalawāt prescribed by the mashāikh of the Shādhilliyya Tariqa is profuse. The reason for doing so is that it creates a nūr in the heart that guides towards good. In a way it is an alternative to having a sheikh kāmil. However, there is a considerable difference between the badl (alternative) and the aṣl (original source) i.e. having a sheikh. This spiritual link, exist from the first generation of Islām until our time. So, this chain of transmission (of Islāmic spirituality) is the original source.

One should be mindful of the rewards of ṣalawāt by reading the book *Faḍāil Durūd*. Also, one's intention should also be corrected, one should adhere to the sunna and make masnūn duʿā specific to the situation. For this one should read the book *al-Utūr al-Majmūʿa*.[179]

---

178 A fiqh text for the average Muslim according to the Ḥanafi tradition.
179 Another book by the author, written in Urdu in which he combined Maulāna Ashraf ʿAli Thānwi's ﷺ 'Nashrut Ṭīb' and Haḍrat Sheikh Maulāna Zakariyya's ﷺ 'Khasāil Nabawi'. The first is a sīra book

مُنْجِيَات

These seven verses of the Qurān are known as Munjiyāt. They have been proven to be a shield from various hardships and difficulties from the experiences of ʿAllāma ibn Sirīn رَحِمَهُ ٱللَّه.

بسم الله الرحمن الرحيم

قُل لَّن يُصِيبَنَآ إِلَّا مَا كَتَبَ ٱللَّهُ لَنَا هُوَ مَوْلَىٰنَا وَعَلَى ٱللَّهِ فَلْيَتَوَكَّلِ ٱلْمُؤْمِنُونَ ۞

بسم الله الرحمن الرحيم

وَإِن يَمْسَسْكَ ٱللَّهُ بِضُرٍّ فَلَا كَاشِفَ لَهُ إِلَّا هُوَ وَإِن يُرِدْكَ بِخَيْرٍ فَلَا رَآدَّ لِفَضْلِهِ يُصِيبُ بِهِ مَن يَشَآءُ مِنْ عِبَادِهِ وَهُوَ ٱلْغَفُورُ ٱلرَّحِيمُ ۞

بسم الله الرحمن الرحيم

وَمَا مِن دَآبَّةٍ فِي ٱلْأَرْضِ إِلَّا عَلَى ٱللَّهِ رِزْقُهَا وَيَعْلَمُ مُسْتَقَرَّهَا وَمُسْتَوْدَعَهَا كُلٌّ فِي كِتَابٍ مُّبِينٍ ۞

---

while the second is about the characteristics and qualities of our beloved Prophet ﷺ. As far as known to the translator there is no English translation as yet.

بسم الله الرحمن الرحيم

إِنِّي تَوَكَّلْتُ عَلَى اللهِ رَبِّي وَرَبِّكُم مَّا مِن دَآبَّةٍ إِلَّا هُوَ آخِذٌ بِنَاصِيَتِهَا إِنَّ رَبِّي عَلَى صِرَاطٍ مُّسْتَقِيمٍ ۞

بسم الله الرحمن الرحيم

وَكَأَيِّن مِّن دَآبَّةٍ لَّا تَحْمِلُ رِزْقَهَا اللهُ يَرْزُقُهَا وَإِيَّاكُمْ وَهُوَ السَّمِيعُ الْعَلِيمُ ۞

بسم الله الرحمن الرحيم

مَا يَفْتَحِ اللهُ لِلنَّاسِ مِن رَّحْمَةٍ فَلَا مُمْسِكَ لَهَا وَمَا يُمْسِكْ فَلَا مُرْسِلَ لَهُ مِن بَعْدِهِ وَهُوَ الْعَزِيزُ الْحَكِيمُ ۞

بسم الله الرحمن الرحيم

وَلَئِن سَأَلْتَهُم مَّنْ خَلَقَ السَّمَوَاتِ وَالْأَرْضَ لَيَقُولُنَّ اللهُ قُلْ أَفَرَأَيْتُم مَّا تَدْعُونَ مِن دُونِ اللهِ إِنْ أَرَادَنِيَ اللهُ بِضُرٍّ هَلْ هُنَّ كَاشِفَاتُ ضُرِّهِ أَوْ أَرَادَنِي بِرَحْمَةٍ هَلْ هُنَّ مُمْسِكَاتُ رَحْمَتِهِ قُلْ حَسْبِيَ اللهُ عَلَيْهِ يَتَوَكَّلُ الْمُتَوَكِّلُونَ ۞

تمّت